T0383705

"In his book, *Managing the COVID-19 Pandemic in South Korea: Policy Learning Perspectives*, Kilkon Ko provides a thoughtful, well-documented analysis of how South Korea, as a democratic country, managed the COVID-19 pandemic using a flexible, informed strategy that relied largely on voluntary cooperation with an informed civil society instead of mandatory, hierarchical controls. This is a powerful analysis that presents insights gained from South Korea's responsible management of this global threat that will inform other nations in other global threats that will surely come."

**Louise K. Comfort**, *Professor Emerita and former Director of the Center for Disaster Management, Graduate School of Public and International Affairs at the University of Pittsburgh, PA, USA*

"In the field of disaster management, the current COVID-19 pandemic has now become a central research theme covering its origins, causes, and remedial strategies. This book systematically covers the widely discussed control mechanisms (e.g., border control, social distancing, and lockdown), explains relevant theoretical approaches, highlights the use of government-citizen interaction and civil society in South Korea, and emphasizes the retention of pandemic-management lessons for facing similar future challenges. This is a very useful book to offer empirically supported arguments and research guidelines for academics and policy makers."

**Professor M. Shamsul Haque**, *National University of Singapore*

"The book uses several perspectives, theories, and frameworks from emergency and crisis management in examining Korea's successful response to COVID-19. Several frameworks were utilized because of the complexity of the COVID-19 response by the government as well as partnership with other stakeholders and members of society. The book highlights collaborative governance, transparent risk communication, and effective lessons learned from MERS experience as core success factors in response. The book is an important resource for scholars, practitioners, and policymakers."

**Naim Kapucu, PhD**, *Pegasus Professor, School of Public Administration & School of Politics, Security, and International Affairs, University of Central Florida (UCF)*

# Managing the COVID-19 Pandemic in South Korea

This book examines the importance of accumulated disaster management experience and the risk awareness of civil society by analyzing Korea's COVID-19 response from the perspective of policy learning. Prior to the spread of COVID-19, Korea was a country with active exchange with China, with over six million Chinese visitors and over five million Korean visitors to China. Korea also has the highest population density among OECD countries and an urbanization rate exceeding 90%, making it vulnerable to the spread of infectious diseases. However, Korea had very low fatality and infection rates among OECD countries, despite foregoing border closures or city lockdowns.

Korea is known as a representative example of state-led economic development called the developmental state model. However, Korea's COVID-19 response emphasizes citizen-led efforts, the use of information and communication technology, and successful disease control through cooperation between the government and civil society. This book presents examples that demonstrate the effectiveness of disaster response based on democratic values, by enhancing the capacity of civil society through social interaction resulting from various models such as rational models, heuristics, cooperative governance, policy networks, and complex adaptive systems. Additionally, it argues that the lesson learned from Korea's COVID-19 experience is not that a strong state should control citizens' freedom to increase the effectiveness of disease control, but rather that sharing the awareness of the risk enables voluntary citizen responses and solidarity consciousness of civil society is essential.

The book is a useful reference for anyone interested in learning more about the value of actors in policy networks.

**Kilkon Ko** is Professor at the Graduate School of Public Administration, Asia Regional Information Center, Asia Center, Seoul National University, South Korea.

# Routledge Focus on Public Governance in Asia

*Series Editors:*
**Hong Liu**, *Nanyang Technological University, Singapore*
**Wenxuan Yu**, *Xiamen University, China*

Focusing on new governance challenges, practices and experiences in and about a globalizing Asia, particularly East Asia and Southeast Asia, this focus series invites upcoming and established researchers all over the world to succinctly and comprehensively discuss important public administration and policy themes such as government administrative reform, public budgeting reform, government crisis management, public–private partnership, science and technology policy, technology-enabled public service delivery, public health and aging, talent management, and anti-corruption across Asian countries. The book series presents compact and concise content under 50,000 words long which has significant theoretical contributions to the governance theory with an Asian perspective and practical implications for administration and policy reform and innovation.

**Sustainable Development Goal 3**
Health and Well-being of Ageing in Hong Kong
*Ben Y. F. Fong and Vincent T. S. Law*

**Mainland China's Taiwan Policy**
From Peaceful Development to Selective Engagement
*Xin Qiang*

**Public Administration and Governance in China**
Chinese Insights with Global Perspectives
*Leizhen Zang and Yanyan Gao*

**The Nature of Japanese Governance and Seikai-Tensin in Postwar Japan**
*Nara Park*

**Managing the COVID-19 Pandemic in South Korea**
Policy Learning Perspectives
*Kilkon Ko*

For more information about this series, please visit www.routledge.com/Routledge-Focus-on-Public-Governance-in-Asia/book-series/RFPGA

# Managing the COVID-19 Pandemic in South Korea

Policy Learning Perspectives

**Kilkon Ko**

Routledge
Taylor & Francis Group

LONDON AND NEW YORK

First published 2023
by Routledge
4 Park Square, Milton Park, Abingdon, Oxon, OX14 4RN

and by Routledge
605 Third Avenue, New York, NY 10158

*Routledge is an imprint of the Taylor & Francis Group, an informa business*

*British Library Cataloguing-in-Publication Data*
A catalogue record for this book is available from the British Library

ISBN: 9780367645373 (hbk)
ISBN: 9780367645403 (pbk)
ISBN: 9781003125006 (ebk)

DOI: 10.4324/9781003125006

Typeset in Times New Roman
by Deanta Global Publishing Services, Chennai, India

Dedicated to my parents and parents-in-law who sacrifice their lives for their children

.

This book is supported by 2023 book grant of the Korean Institute of Public Affairs, Seoul National University.

# Contents

# Figures

# Tables

# Preface

The impact of COVID-19 was something the world had never experienced before, and each country responded differently. Existing disaster management studies have emphasized the importance of communication and coordination and argued that international cooperation is a crucial success factor in responding to disasters. However, ChatGPT, a device that uses a massive corpus of text data to find patterns and relationships, cites New Zealand, Taiwan, and Vietnam as countries that responded most effectively to COVID-19, and suggests 'strict border control' as a common success factor. While border control is not the only factor, many people have expressed that more robust border control and social distancing policies were the success factor of the COVID-19 response. If this is the case, when new disasters occur in the future, it is likely that disaster management will take the form of stronger control and be justified by this former COVID-19 experience. Should this turn out to be the case, our lessons from COVID-19 will be a serious threat to democracy and the freedom of citizens. Rather than hastily concluding what we have done during the pandemic era, there is a need to reexamine and rediscover the various responses and lessons that we may have overlooked. This book analyzes the case of Korea's response to COVID-19. Various evaluations have been made regarding Korea's response, but existing studies have arguably given excessive attention to the 3T (trace–test–treat) policy, which is commonly understood as the success factor of 'K-Quarantine'. However, the interaction between citizens and government from conducting this policy and the impacts of doing so are overlooked. Most importantly, the response model based on citizen autonomy is little discussed when reviewing the Korean model. In Korea, border closing was not implemented, but quarantine measures for entrants strengthened the response, and the spread of COVID-19 was controlled without significantly reducing the mobility of citizens and without locking down the city. Additionally, despite concerns about the side effects of vaccination, more than 90% of citizens chose to be vaccinated rapidly. The violation of the self-quarantine rule was less than 1%, and panic-buying did not happen despite the shortage of personal hygiene product supply.

The central argument of this book is that effective responses to COVID-19 in Korea were not simply because of substantial government control.

Administrative systems in Asian countries are still primarily misunderstood as authoritarian and centralized. Of course, China maintains an authoritarian government system to the extent that the leadership of the Communist Party is stipulated in Article 1 of the Constitution. The zero-covid policy is acceptable in China, but this is not politically feasible in Korea, Japan, and Taiwan, which have developed into democratic systems. Compared to European countries that opted to enforce city blockades, Korea, Japan, and Taiwan did not adopt a city blockade policy. As for the social distancing policy, in Korea, a whole community approach was taken to recognize and solve the problem while involving various actors in the policy process. In responding to COVID-19, Korea, with its limitations, constantly pondered over democratic values and the role of civil society. There were opinions in favor of a strong social distancing policy even within Korea, but the citizens chose a quarantine policy based on autonomy.

This book applies various disaster management frameworks to Korea's response to COVID-19 because no single framework is enough to understand the complex responses of Korean society. Despite the complexity of understanding disaster management, one thing is clear: collaboration with multiple actors, transparency and risk communication, utilizing information communication technology and other medical technical services, public-private collaboration, and civil society are crucial factors. In addition to these factors, this book points out that past experiences and lessons learned from the MERS experiences profoundly impacted Korea's response to COVID-19; thus, it is critical to reexamine and reflect on the memories and lessons learned from COVID-10 experiences.

The purpose of this book goes beyond outlining Korea's response to COVID-19. The broader motivation of this book is to reflect on what Korea experienced and learned from responding to COVID-19 to gain various ideas as we move into the future. This is because as time passes, what we need to learn regarding COVID-19 can easily be forgotten, with important memories distorted. This book was written by referring to the various models to explain the phenomenon rather than trying to explain the phenomenon to fit a complex disaster model.

This book underwent several revision processes. I had no choice but to revise the manuscript several times, especially the earlier drafts, as COVID-19 unexpectedly progressed for over three years. In this process, I realized why reflecting on disaster management through one lens is impossible. I came to understand the importance and value of collaborating with many people, especially for a book project like this one. I am indebted to Louise K. Comfort, Mary Lee Rhodes, and other colleagues who contributed to the book *Global Risk Management: The Role of Collective Cognition in Response to COVID-19* through nearly two years of meetings and collaborations. The conversations we shared were of crucial importance. The contents of Ko, Chang, and Lee's (2022), "The Impact of Inter-Crisis Learning on the Risk Cognition and the Utilization of Information Technologies in Korea", which was published through this work, were referred to in this manuscript.

A special thank you to Dr. Saemi Chang for helping to supply the theoretical framework and Dr. Hyunjae Shin for contributing to the research related to the lockdown policy. I would also like to express my gratitude to Minjun Hong, Kyungdong Kim, and Bum Kim, as well as the Seoul National University's Graduate School of Public Administration research students who collected and analyzed the COVID-19-related data. Thank you also to Dr. Minjae Zoh for reading this manuscript from beginning to end and providing comments. The Asia Regional Information Center at Seoul National University Asia Center where I serve as a director has also greatly helped me systematically collect and analyze COVID-19 data and policies.

I would also like to wholeheartedly thank Professor John Mendeloff, who has guided and encouraged me since my doctorate studies. Last but certainly not least, I would like to thank the editorial staff at Routledge for their patience and understanding despite the delays in completing this book due to the ongoing COVID-19 re-proliferation.

Kilkon Ko
Seoul National University

# 1  Introduction

When reports of unknown pneumonia were released in Wuhan, China, the Republic of Korea (hereafter Korea) health authority escalated the surveillance for pneumonia cases in health facilities nationwide on January 3, 2020 (Comfort et al., 2020). That same day, the Korean government enhanced the quarantine and screening measures for travelers from Wuhan at the point of entry (PoE). Few people at the time could predict that this unknown pneumonia (soon to be coined COVID-19) would grow into a global pandemic, causing millions of deaths, immeasurable costs, and unprecedented social distancing policies globally and locally.

Even when the first confirmed case was reported on January 20, 2020, very few expected that COVID-19 would last longer than three years. When COVID-19 broke out in China, Korea was immediately an area of concern for exposure and contamination due to its geographical proximity to China. More than six million Chinese people visited Korea in 2019, the norm as China was Korea's largest trade partner. The trade volumes between the two countries were more than US$280 billion in 2019. It is important to remember that Korea is a highly populated country with a population of over 50 million. Due to its rapid urbanization, more than 25 million people live in the capital area of Seoul, which also means that this area is much more vulnerable and open to infectious diseases like COVID-19. Moreover, Korea is highly connected to the world. Incheon Airport was ranked the fifth largest airport worldwide and dealt with more than 70 million international travelers in 2019. Given this condition, there was no doubt that the COVID-19 crisis in China would be an imminent threat to Korea. Despite this expected risk, it can be argued that Korea responded to COVID-19 effectively.

Transparency was an issue from the beginning. Along with the worldwide spread of COVID-19, an unprecedentedly firm quarantine policy caused by ignorance and fear began to spread worldwide. In hindsight, one can say that China's initial response could have been more effective. China did not actively communicate the risks of COVID-19 to the public during its early stages. What was happening in Wuhan was a bit mysterious to the outside world, leading to other countries having doubts about the statistics being released on infection and death rates. The Korean government attempted to

DOI: 10.4324/9781003125006-1

share information as transparently as possible. Former U.S. President Donald Trump claimed he could not trust Korea's COVID-19 death toll statistics to defend his administration's handling of the pandemic on July 28, 2018.[1] At the time, Korea had 300 deaths out of a population of 50 million. The death rate per 100,000 in Korea was 0.6, but that of the United States. was 48.3. Contrary to Mr. Trump, there were few doubts from the Korean public that the government was manipulating statistics, as all information was transparently released twice a day at designated times. Notably, a large percentage of the Korean public showed continuous support for the Korean government's COVID-19 response, especially for its transparent policy. According to the Gallop Korea Daily Opinion Poll survey shown in Figure 1.1, more than half of the Korean people supported the government regarding their COVID-19 response.

The liberal response approach of Korea is also notable. Korea did not have any form of lockdown of cities or full-scale border closures. In 2020, many cities worldwide, especially the ones that were densely populated, decided to go into lockdown. Furthermore, the movement of people became restricted, and patients suspected of being infected were thoroughly quarantined. On March 26, 2020, China closed its border and prohibited the entry of foreign nationals or resident permit holders after the announcement by the Ministry of Foreign Affairs and the National Immigration Administration on the temporary suspension of entry by foreign nationals holding valid Chinese visas or residence

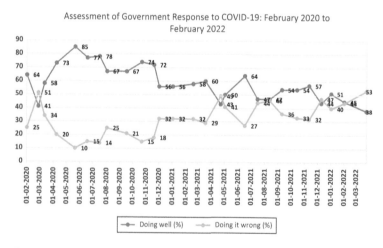

*Figure 1.1* Opinion polls on the 'Support of Government's COVID-19 responses. Assessment of government responses to COVID-19: February 2020 to February 2022. Suggested as of the investigation end date. Biweekly in February 2020, phone survey of about 1,000 adults nationwide for three days per time point once a month from March – Gallup Korea Daily Opinion No. 482 www.gallup.co.kr

permits. While the United States and some countries criticized the Chinese approach as an authoritarian one, limiting freedom of travel, they also adopted border closure and lockdown policies. The state exerted unprecedented power by restricting the freedom of travel, and the right to have proper education, which, in turn, affected the quality of education, the right to carry out business, as well as the right to privacy. The return of the 'big government' was permitted in the name of the war on COVID-19. Interestingly, Korea chose a different path from China and other countries. For example, Korea did not adopt full-scale border closure. Korea allowed most international travelers' entry to Korea under the condition that all travelers had to fulfill a two-week quarantine. The only restriction that the Korean government made was for those entering from heavily infected areas in China and other countries. Such an approach was supported due to the emphasis on democratic values in the Korean society.

There was no mandatory business ban, and the public transportation system operated. Interestingly, the infection and death cases of COVID-19 in Korea were significantly small compared to other countries in Europe and North America. An impressive fact is that Korea did not lock down any of its cities. Protective face masks were offered to citizens despite significant supply shortages. Voluntary civilian experts and private companies made public health resources more accessible. They helped people to locate stocked pharmacies and orderly distribute masks using the real-time mask inventory open API (application programming interface) data provided by the government. The citizens' compliance with social distancing policies was so high that most wore face masks and followed the restriction to gatherings. The 3T (testing, tracing, and treatment) strategy adopted by Korea was recognized as one of the best practices in the world by WHO, ADB, and global mass media. As a result, among the 50 million people, there were 917 confirmed death cases by January 1, 2021, in Korea, a considerably lower death rate than in other countries. Also, the economic shock was arguably managed well. The OECD evaluated the financial performance of Korea as follows:

> The Korean economy withstood the blow dealt by COVID-19 better than most, with one of the smallest contractions in economic output of any OECD country – and its GDP per capita surpassing the OECD average for the first time. This underlines Korea's skillful management of the pandemic.
>
> (In Focus: OECD ECONOMIC Survey of Korea, 2022)

Some may argue that Korea's success was due to the characteristics of an authoritarian government observed among Asian countries, but unlike China, which decided to pursue an excessively enforcing quarantine policy, Korea, Japan, and Singapore agreed to implement a reasonably flexible quarantine policy. There is a misunderstanding that the high mask-wearing or vaccination rates shown in these countries resulted from authoritarian coercion. However, even before the government officially imposed mask-wearing regulations, or after lifting the regulations, many Koreans and Japanese voluntarily wore masks. Despite concerns about vaccines, high vaccination rates were demonstrated. On the contrary, the government, which had low trust in citizens' autonomy, restricted unvaccinated people from using restaurants or public facilities. This resulted in infringing on citizens' freedom, especially those who could not take vaccines due to personal health issues.

There is much hindsight that Korea has experienced from this. First, Korea had and remained to have difficulty returning to its pre-COVID-19 routine because of its risk-averse policy. Until the end of 2022, Korea did not lift the mandatory facial mask-wearing regulation indoors because many of the bureaucrats did not want to take responsibility for the insurgence of infection cases after lifting the regulation. Second, political criticism was sometimes groundlessly raised. The politicization of COVID-19 responses is to the use of the pandemic for political gain, rather than addressing it in a neutral and scientifically based manner. This can lead to biased decision-making, unequal allocation of resources, and mistrust in the government's handling of the crisis. The consequences of politicizing a public health emergency can be severe and undermine the efforts to control the spread of the disease and protect public health. In Korea, the conservative party, People's Power Party, criticized the government's policy as a politicized-quarantine policy in 2021 but the party continued similar policies even after it won the presidential election in 2022. The progressive government also showed a double standard attitude by hostile negative groups' gatherings for pandemic prevention while remaining silent about meetings of pro-government groups.

Third, the central government still wants to control local governments. When local governments attempted to relax the epidemic prevention standards independently, the central government criticized them for not being fair with other regions. It required them to follow the central government's policy. As a result, some local governments, which had less population and small infection cases, could lift the facial mask policy. Even during the early stage of COVID-19, some local governments whose infection cases were minimal could not voluntarily decide whether to reopen offline classes.

This book explores the Korean case, and the aims are twofold. The first is to review how Korea has responded to COVID-19 over the past three years. The second is to look back on mistakes made to avoid them in the future. The reflection has been made based on the role of government and other actors, the importance of scientific information and technologies, and resilient civil society. Academics have discussed how to respond to the disaster which has been a critical question for a long time. As Charles Perrow has argued, we face many accidents that cause multiple and unexpected failures built into a society that consists of complex and tightly coupled systems (Perrow, 1984). Because of such complexities, disaster management is framed as a complex adaptive system (Comfort, 1999; Hodges & Larra, 2021) or response network (Moynihan, 2008). It emphasizes the collaboration among actors and communities in the system or network. The idea is consistent with the emphasis on collaborative governance (Ansell & Gash, 2008; Crosby & Bryson, 2005), which attempts to replace the managerial and authoritarian mode of public administration and policymaking. This approach is based on the reflection that new public management (Ferlie 1996, Barzelay 2001) restoring managerial efficiency is insufficient to solve complex problems as a democratic society pursues diverse and competing public values (Denhardt & Denhardt, 2015; Fukumoto & Bozeman, 2019). Before the COVID-19 pandemic, the market, community, and citizens seemed to be at the core of dealing with social problems.

Unlike the emphasis on democratic governance before COVID-19 broke out, interestingly, we observed the return of strong or even authoritarian government metaphors around the world during the response to COVID-19. Governments have adopted aggressive policies such as lockdown of cities, closing borders and schools, tracking individual movements despite the privacy issue, imposing regulations on wearing a mask, and spending billions of dollars for relief subsidies. The state-centric and hierarchical approach is a dominant framework in the COVID-19 response. It is important to note that authoritarianism is not unique to Asia and is also not a cultural characteristic of the region. Rather, it is the result of historical, political, and economic factors and the choices made by political leaders and societies. The Korean public administration, usually known for having Confucius and hierarchical management style, has responded to COVID-19 by abiding by democratic principles emphasizing collaboration with civil society.

## Note

1 *Yonhap News*, "Trump suggests S. Korea's coronavirus death toll can't be trusted", August 05, 2020.

# 2 Overview of the Evolution of COVID-19 in Korea

Korea managed to record zero confirmed cases during the SARS epidemic in 2002. As for the Middle East Respiratory Syndrome (MERS) epidemic in 2015, it carried out quarantine measures while minimizing the number of confirmed cases to 186 and deaths to 38 by quickly resolving the problem of initial hospital cluster infection. Having undergone such experiences, many experts believed that they could control COVID-19 during the early phases of the disease.

When COVID-19 first started to spread, no one predicted it would go on for such a long time. Since the first case was confirmed on January 20, 2020, the number of confirmed cases was very small. The Koreans mistakenly believed that they had successfully controlled COVID-19, unlike China's response. In the social milieu, even President Moon Jae-in argued on February 13 that the COVID-19 problem would not last too long. However, the second outbreak of COVID-19 started on February 17 due to the Shincheonji (religious cult group) community infections in the Daegu City. The upsurge of confirmed cases until mid-March was mainly because of the second-wave shock related to Shincheonji holding a massive gathering in Daegu City. One might argue that community infection in such a religious group would be negligible. However, more than 80% of total infections in Korea by the end of March 2020 were directly or indirectly related to it.

However, much like other countries, Korea also went through several spread patterns of the disease. The first panel of Figure 2.1 shows the trend of new confirmed cases of COVID-19 from January 2020 to May 2022. From this data, we can learn that the point in time when the number of new confirmed cases was most high was March 2022 with days when the number of confirmed cases exceeded 621,328. On the other hand, the trend of new confirmed cases before 2022 appears to have undergone no change according to the first panel of Figure 2.1. However, this is not the actual case. Figure 2.1 shows the trend of the seven-day moving average of confirmed cases in 2020, 2021, and 2022, respectively, and it is possible to see how there were considerable fluctuations per year. Looking first at the cases of 2020 in Korea, the number of new confirmed cases per day did not exceed 4,000 until October 2020. Compared to March 2022, the number of new confirmed cases at this

DOI: 10.4324/9781003125006-2

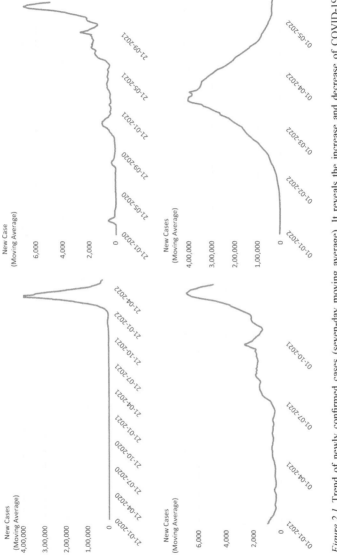

*Figure 2.1* Trend of newly confirmed cases (seven-day moving average). It reveals the increase and decrease of COVID-19 confirmed cases. *Source:* KCDC, Asia Regional Information Center, SNUAC.

time can be seen to be insignificant. However, the fear of COVID-19 was indeed alarming. In 2020, schools adopted a very strong quarantine policy and this involved switching to online classes, closing the entire building when a confirmed case occurred, or requiring mandatory quarantine at medical facilities for ten days. On the other hand, in 2022, the number of cases was high, but social distancing restrictions in schools and restaurants were almost lifted and the confirmed patients revealed a reduced number, and hospitalization was changed to self-quarantine. Despite the level of confirmed cases being a few thousand times more than in 2020, the level of social distancing was lowered. What the COVID-19 phenomenon over the past three years shows is that we should not judge the severity of the pandemic simply by the absolute change in the number of confirmed cases. The diagnosis and prescription for the situation inevitably change according to the context the virus is in progress.

Figure 2.1 also reveals that the increase and decrease in COVID-19 confirmed cases consistently repeat each year. When the COVID-19 vaccine was approved in December 2020, and vaccination began on February 26, 2021, many people expected that the virus would decrease at a rapid pace. However, even when vaccination rates exceeded 80% in Korea, the Omicron mutation spread in January 2022 was much more extensive than before. Interestingly, fear of the spread of COVID-19 has been reduced, despite the increase in confirmed cases. As such, it is necessary to understand the disaster process as a dynamically changing process rather than a simple linear process of occurrence spread, reduction, and termination, and it should be noted that the size and intensity of the risk are relative. Considering that the bureaucracy responding to disasters has high rigidity and high path dependency, it can be said that the importance of disaster response governance that constantly monitors the dynamically changing COVID-19 situation and enables policies is substantial.

The change in the fatality rate, defined as the ratio of death cases to confirmed cases, also shows the stable and efficient medical service in Korea. First, as shown in Figure 2.2, the European Union and North America show the highest fatality rate in the early stage of 2020. The high fatality rate in the EU and North America was due to many deaths in early convalescent hospitals, but it is noteworthy that the fatality rate was low in Korea, which also had a high level of aging and a very high population density. Another point to note is that the African continent's fatality rate was relatively low compared to the EU or North America in the early days, but due to the underdeveloped medical environment, the fatality rate steadily maintained at more than 2% from 2022. Second, Korea was able to maintain a consistently lower fatality rate compared to other OECD countries, not only by lowering the fatality rate during the early stages of the COVID-19 pandemic. Korea not only showed its capability in the early response but also demonstrated excellent crisis management skills in the subsequent stages.

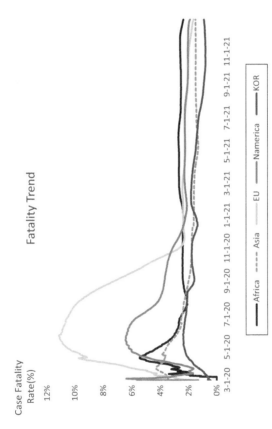

*Figure 2.2* Fatality trend. *Source:* Our World in Data.

As the trend in the confirmation rate and fatality rate shows, Korea prevented the spread through prompt response from the beginning and was able to reduce the fatality rate by providing appropriate medical services to confirmed patients. Korea's low confirmation and fatality rates are different from China's. While China controlled the spread of COVID-19 based on strong social distancing policies such as border closures and extensive movement restrictions, Korea effectively controlled COVID-19 without prompting policies such as border closures, or restrictions on movement, which is indeed a big difference. Additionally, there was little social conflict or corruption in the provision of medical services, from mask supply to vaccination. Furthermore, the economic impact was also effectively absorbed.

Figure 2.3 shows the 2020 real GDP growth rates of major countries. From the real GDP growth rates in 2020, one can see that most countries record a minus growth rate, except for some countries such as Ireland and China. However, 2021 shows a significant positive growth rate due to the base effect of 2020.

Korea's economic shock during COVID-19 reveals a stable yet rapid recovery. As can be seen in Figure 2.4, Korea achieved -0.4% real GDP growth in 2020, mitigating the economic shock much better than the United Kingdom or Spain's -11% growth rate, and achieved a high growth rate of 4.1% in 2021. This suggests that factory closures and contraction in the service industry were relatively small. Korea's trade dependency measured as

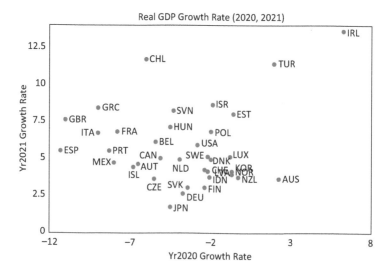

*Figure 2.3* The real GDP growth rate of OECD and other major countries. *Source:* Our World in Data.

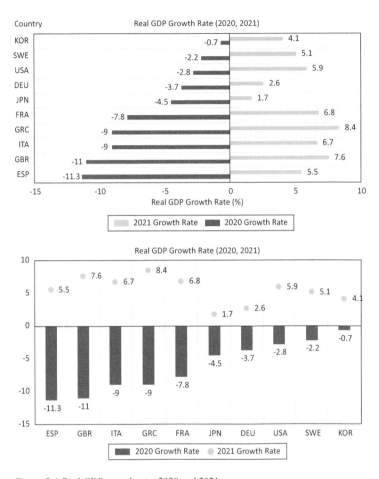

*Figure 2.4* Real GDP growth rate: 2020 and 2021.

a percentage of the trade volume to the GDP was around 69.2% in 2020. Despite being a country highly dependent on external trade, ranking ninth in the world in 2019, Korea responded well to the COVID-19 economic crisis without a sudden decrease in domestic consumption or trade.

What should be noted in response to COVID-19 is that the virus is a respiratory infectious disease agent, and deaths predominantly occur in the elderly population. The left side of Figure 2.5 shows the age distribution of cumulative deaths from COVID-19 until December 31, 2020. Korea's total population is about 50 million, but at the time, the cumulative number of COVID-19 deaths until December 31, 2020, was only 900. More than 95% of these deaths

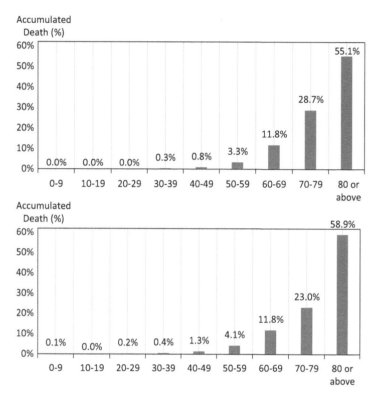

*Figure 2.5* The percentage of death by age (December 31, 2020; May 31, 2022).
*Source:* KCDC, Asia Regional Information Center, SNUAC.

were among elderly people over the age of 60. This did not change significantly even when the Delta mutations and Omicron mutations spread thereafter. The figure on the right shows the cumulative COVID-19 death rate by age
on May 31, 2022, revealing that only 6.1% of the 24,176 deaths were under
the age of 60. In the end, COVID-19 deaths in the early days of COVID-19 or
thereafter, a lot of versions of mutations occurred, mainly in the elderly, and
this can be said to be due to the characteristics of COVID-19 as a respiratory
disease. Suppose a pandemic in the future emerges and is a different type of
infectious disease, such as a digestive or vascular rather than a respiratory
disease. In that case, there may be a different type of spread pattern and vulnerable age group compared to COVID-19.

Korea's high vaccination rate is also noteworthy. Korea started vaccination on February 26, 2021, and it began with the elderly and health care workers over the age of 65. Despite the fear of the side effects of the vaccine, Korea

had already exceeded 80% of vaccine recipients at the end of October 21, 2021, and the elderly group who had been vaccinated first had a vaccination rate of over 90%. Considering that the rate of full vaccination by the end of 2022 in the United States was only 65%, Korea's vaccination rate can be said to be very high. It is also worth noting that the vaccination was conducted at a fast pace which showed Korea's medical capacity to quickly administer the vaccine to the entire population. Some may misunderstand that such rapid vaccination was possible because there are many government-led public medical institutions like in China. However, in Korea, the ratio of private to government medical institutions is over 94%, much higher than the OECD average of 44.5%. The key to efficiency is not whether it is public or private, but how the process of providing health care is systematically linked through collaboration among sectors. While Korea adopts the national health insurance system, treatment services are provided by private hospitals, and information on prescriptions and medical costs is collected and shared through the government's integrated medical information system, so it is well-connected in an emergency such as COVID-19. In particular, the process of application for vaccination, confirmation of vaccination, and notification of additional vaccinations were managed through a computer system, and this was all possible by connecting and managing not only patients in public hospitals but also patients who had been vaccinated in private hospitals (Figure 2.6).

The prompt provision of disaster relief funds is also noteworthy. In May 2020, the Korean government provided disaster relief funds of $400 for single-person households and $1,000 for four-person households, and this was to all citizens. In order to pay disaster subsidies to all citizens, the government

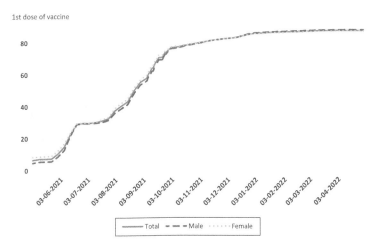

*Figure 2.6* COVID-19 vaccination trend. *Source:* Asia Regional Information Center, SNUAC.

had to identify the individual's residence and financial information. Obtaining this information inevitably takes significant time and administrative costs. To cope with the challenge, the Korean government collaborated with the credit card companies so that the disaster subsidy could be received in the form of a credit or debit card, and thus individuals could quickly apply online. From the perspective of the bank, it is profitable to use the subsidy using the company's credit card, so they made a website and promoted it so that customers could easily apply for the subsidy. In order to prevent system overload, a method of sequentially applying the application date according to one's birth month was also used. Additionally, for the elderly who found it difficult to make online applications, the local governments identified the nonapplicants and visited the elderly or the disabled. Such a visiting service was possible because many elderly people were receiving various welfare services such as a basic pension or health insurance and so they were identified and accessible using the welfare system.

The COVID-19 response process should not simply be perceived from the government's point of view. Through the MERS response process in 2015, Korea began to recognize disaster response as a matter of responding to society as a whole from the perspective of individual subjects. However, as Ha (2016) explained, MERS enabled the Korean government to realize the importance of the prevention of community infection and a holistic approach to coordinating different actors at different stages, rather than ordering or controlling them, as shown in Figure 2.7. The prevention of community infection cannot be achieved by the government alone but by an intensive level of cooperation by sharing information, resources, and goals. COVID-19 posed

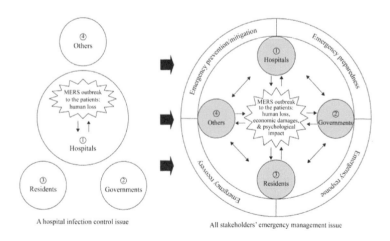

*Figure 2.7* Paradigm change of responses to MERS in Korea. *Source:* Ha (2016).

not only health risks to a wider range of people compared to MERS, but also economic and psychological risks, making the importance of cooperation between hospitals, small businesses, educational institutions, and various civic organizations even greater.

Response to epidemics consists of multiple actors and complex activities at different stages. Even if there is a small error in tens of activities, the effectiveness of the response system is heavily damaged. After overcoming MERS, the Korean government published a white paper on the response to MERS in Korea. In the white paper, the Korean government identified the following components as key factors to consider for responding to epidemics (Table 2.1).

Local government, officials, hospitals, social welfare institutions, educational institutions, and others who have to implement government policies on the ground face various situations. If their decision-making is left to individual discretion, it damages the consistency and predictability of policies. In particular, due to the characteristics of bureaucracy, if specific guidelines are not provided, there is a tendency to use the resources and authority granted passively. Therefore, providing consistent guidelines is necessary. With this awareness, the Korean government has continuously revised its response guidelines based on the problems identified during the COVID-19 response process, for hospitals, local governments, educational institutions, and local governments. Hence, the Korean government has provided various guidelines to address COVID-19, including guidelines for the safe management of related waste, quarantine measures, medical institution response, hospitalization treatment cost guidelines, operation guidelines for rehabilitation centers, guidelines for local governments, and a manual for responding to infectious diseases for people with disabilities. These guidelines are continuously updated and shared when new issues are identified by experts, streetlevel bureaucrats, and other implementation agencies.

*Table 2.1* Component of major activities for managing MERS

- Structuring response governance
- Quarantine
- Epidemiological surveillance
- Infection tests
- Risk communication
- Managing contacts
- Intensive management of hospitals
- Triage and treatment of infected patients
- Supports and compensations
- International cooperation

*Source:* Ministry of Health and Welfare (2016), "The 2015 MERS outbreak in the Republic of Korea: Learning from MERS".

# 3 Theoretical Frameworks for Understanding Disaster Management

COVID-19 has proven to be an unstructured, uncertain, and cross-border issue, which makes us realize the limitations of rational problem-solving with professional scientific knowledge (Lindblom & Cohen, 1979; Wildavsky, 1979). Many countries lacked sufficient information on how the disease would cause unprecedented threats to global society at its early stage. Even China, heavily hit by COVID-19 earlier than other countries, did not have enough information on how to respond to this unprecedented infectious disease. The fatality rate, transmission mechanism, and asymptomatic patient rate were not readily available in early February 2020, and WHO did not have enough information to make other countries prepare. As the result, the global response to COVID-19 was delayed due to insufficient information. European countries and the United States failed to control the disease in March 2020. Following this, Latin American countries, Russia, and India were overwhelmed by COVID-19 in the following months. While we believed that lockdown of a city, vaccinations, and intensive social distancing policies would be a solution to end the pandemic, such expectations were not materialized properly. The reality was that we continually became exposed to the uprise of new waves of COVID-19 infections.

Such failure is not simply because of the absence of rational policymaking efforts. Many countries have their own disaster management systems designed for the prevention, preparedness, response, and recovery of disasters. Few of them, however, expect a pandemic like COVID-19, and the disaster management system did not work satisfactorily in this particular case. In 2020, most countries employed high-level social distancing measures, including the lockdown of cities, travel restrictions, border shutdown, and school closure, but these measures did not prove to be as effective as anticipated. The global-level failure of the disaster management system is perplexing in that the response system is a result of accumulated scientific knowledge, well-designed institutions, billions of financial resources, and millions of people. Even in developed countries known for having relatively high-quality medical services and well-prepared response systems, COVID-19 caused tremendous damage in its early stages. Hence, why did we fail to respond to COVID-19 despite our recognition of the importance of preparedness? Before answering this question,

DOI: 10.4324/9781003125006-3

we need to review the theoretical framework explaining the efficient disaster management system.

In Korea, the primary keyword dominating the discourse of the disaster response system is the command center called 'control tower' in Korean. One symbolic example is the Sewol ferry sink tragedy in 2014.[1] People believed that the tragedy could have been prevented if the president or the strong control tower exerted its power correctly. After this incident, the Korean government created the Ministry of Public Safety and Security, integrating the public security functions of the Ministry of Security and Public Administration, National Emergency Management Agency, and Korea Coast Guard. The idea that disasters can be overcome by a strong government in a time of uncertainty is attractive, but it does not guarantee that the outcome will always be positive. China's zero-COVID-19 policy seemed to be very effective, but in the end, it caused serious economic problems such as the Shanghai blockade in 2022, and due to the rapid overload of the medical system following the lifting of blockage in 2023, huge social costs had to be paid. There is no empirical evidence that authoritarian states have successfully prevented the spread of COVID-19. But there is thought that a strong government will be able to solve the disaster.

## 3.1 Structural Approaches: Hierarchy versus Policy Network

In the academic literature on disaster management, the most appropriate structure of the disaster management system has been discussed for many years in different contexts. Among them, hierarchical and network structures are widely considered.

### 3.1.1 Hierarchy

The command-and-control paradigm is characterized by hierarchical decision capacities and clear roles (Boersma, 2014). In disaster response organizations, they often set their efforts under the so-called 3-C emergency governance model: assuming that disasters cause 'Chaos', which is managed under 'Control', by means of a 'Command' structure (Quarantelli & Dynes, 1977). Thus, governments tend to rely on measures of control in order to protect social structures and reestablish public order (Tierney et al., 2006). However, the command-and-control paradigm has been criticized by a bulk of researchers in that it is inadequate to enable the flexibility needed during the dynamics of disasters (Moynihan, 2009; Tierney et al., 2006; Curtis, 2008; Boersma, 2014). The inflexibility increases the risk of ignoring local conditions and perspectives. When the decisions are passed up and down the chain of command, critical information is missing and decision-making is delayed. At the same time, as decision-making is centralized, innovation and creativity at the local level are stifled and the existing power structure and control system resist change.

The hierarchical approach emphasizes the restructuring and reorganization of the disaster management system when there is a response failure. For instance, whenever disaster response failure was identified, Korea reorganized the related government agencies. After the Sewol ferry disaster, in 2014, the Ministry of Security and Public Administration changed its name to the Ministry of Public Security and Safety after merging the function of the Korean Coast Guard. Later, after the Gyeongju earthquake in 2016, the Ministry of Public Security and Safety changed its name to the Ministry of Interior and Safety. During the COVID-19 response, the Korean government upgraded the Korea Center for Disease Control to the Korea Disease Control and Prevention.

Such a tendency to rely on formal measures often necessitates a hierarchical structure. Hierarchical structure has the virtue of clarifying the functions and roles of organizations by making it explicit who should take the lead and who else should support operations. Moreover, a hierarchical structure also ensures stability, which enables multiple actors to act rapidly in certain situations. Nonetheless, the very structure may hamper flexibility, which is crucial in disaster management. Ideally, the balance between the two features - stability and flexibility - would enhance effectiveness, but it is not very likely in constantly evolving systems where multiple components form and reform under changing conditions (Comfort, 1999). The stability originated from the hierarchical system preferred by the bureaucracy which heavily relies on rules and documents. Bureaucratic sensemaking is not based on the active interpretation of values but implements the will of their political masters. Hence, the golden rule of bureaucracy is not doing the right thing but doing things right. Such tactical rather than strategic thinking makes the bureaucracy play by the book. In this sense, the bureaucracy within the hierarchical system works very well in normal situations where tasks are well-defined. If we reflect on the millions of tasks done in disaster management, some of them are standardizable through the manuals. For instance, tracking infected patients, vaccinations, allocating medical services, regulating social distancing policies, and distributing relief funds according to manuals are effectively implemented through the hierarchical system. Hence, we can find the success of disaster management based on a hierarchical system when the government deals with well-defined tasks. However, the hierarchical system can be vulnerable if defining problems, searching for solutions, and coordinating different tasks and actors are core tasks of disaster management. In general, these tasks are crucial at the beginning stage of a disaster. It is difficult to process all information through a hierarchical structure in the early stages of a disaster when everything is uncertain, leading to unnecessary delays in immediate response. Therefore, it is more appropriate in many cases to identify and find solutions flexibly on the ground rather than through a hierarchical structure. On the other hand, as information accumulates and repetitive response procedures are established, the effectiveness of response through a hierarchical structure can increase. Hence, disaster management literature proposes alternative disaster management structures such as the policy network framework.

### 3.1.2 Policy Network

Whereas hierarchy addresses structure with rigidity, policy network illustrates structure with more flexibility. A policy network is defined as the relationship formed between the elements of civil society and a government to establish policies (Montpetit, 2002). Interestingly, the term indicates the combination of policy, which is mainly steered by the government, and network, which assumes more horizontal configurations involving various actors. Participants in the policy network interact with each other to achieve the common purpose, or policy goals, developing a structure that impacts outcomes of behavior, concept, attitude, etc. (Marsh & Smith, 2000; Knoke & Kuklinski, 1982).

In a broader sense, the policy network has been conceptualized as an explicit criticism toward 'iron triangles', or 'closed triangles of control' (Heclo, 1978). Though Heclo (1978) used the term "issue network", the idea of having multiple actors who share knowledge in policymaking is the common notion inherent in policy networks. Of course, even within the concept of a policy network, the degrees of relative cohesion, inclusion, and permanence greatly vary according to the research interests, cases, and whatever concept the previous literature chose to use (Enroth, 2011). Whichever approach one chooses, the policy network contains three common characteristics: interdependency, coordination, and pluralism (Enroth, 2011).

Interdependency is a core characteristic of the policy network. While dependency describes a linkage of connection between two entities, interdependency indicates much more complex connections linking multiple points (Rinaldi, Peerenboom, & Kelly, 2001). For instance, when $i$ depends on $j$ and $j$ also depends on $i$ either directly or indirectly, we say $i$ and $j$ are interdependent. The policy network emphasizes mutual dependence rather than a one-way dependency, unlike the hierarchical structure. Mutual dependence is sustainable when the relationship among actors is mutually beneficial. Without such reciprocity, the policy network fails to result in collaboration, and actors would not actively communicate and exchange resources, information, and support. Moreover, the interdependency of the policy network dynamically changes by adding new actors and adjusting the relationship.

When it comes to actual practices, relationships become extremely complex because there are multiple elements interconnected to one another creating an intricate "web" (Rinaldi, Peerenboom, & Kelly, 2001). Since such complex webs of relations are not objectively given by the structure of the network (Enroth, 2011), the challenge for the actors is to make decisions about which outcomes are unpredictable. For instance, in a large-scale disaster such as an earthquake, the very infrastructure systems designed to be efficient under normality may instead efficiently spread danger (Comfort, 1999). This kind of dynamic environment is where each actor in the policy network should establish goals and objectives, construct value systems, model and analyze operations, and make decisions (Rinaldi, Peerenboom, & Kelly, 2001). Unfortunately, shared goals and values are not easily achieved without trust and accumulated experiences of collaboration (Ansell & Gash, 2008). Self-organization is a strong driving force in formulating interdependency, but intentional effort such as coordination is necessary to produce a positive outcome through it.

Another core element of the policy network is coordination. Coordination starts with an assumption that there are differences among actors (Axelrod & Cohen, 1999) and that those actors share a common goal (Comfort, 2007). In the emergency response system, the necessary condition for successful coordination among various actors is the communication that activates the response operations (Comfort, 2007). In order to achieve communication and coordination, the actors should have a "sufficient level of shared information", or in practice, a "common operating picture" (Comfort, 2007). This stresses the importance of sharing key information as a basis for coordinated action. Since the quality of information rather than the quantity of information matters, the data on the time of the demand and severity of the situation facilitates coordination (Comfort et al., 2004). In contrast, the absence of a common operating picture in emergency response operations makes the organizations on the top rely on hierarchical means of control over the lower levels (Comfort, 2007). In a crisis, the critical role of the leaders is to nurture the right conditions (Boint et al., 2005), since coordination is not given, but is both 'a driving force of governance and one of its goals' (Bevir, 2008). Yet, it is not easy even to measure whether or not interactions have occurred among the actors. Ko (2007) suggests clarifying with whom the network participants share resources, what resources they share and why, under what rules, and with what costs and benefits etc. Unless these are discussed in advance, it would be difficult to comprehend how coordination has been achieved.

The pluralist feature underlies interdependency and coordination. After all, without multiple actors, there could not be mutual dependency nor the level of coordination could be acquired. Bevir and Rhodes (2007) note that "a monolithic state in control of itself and civil society was always a myth" because, in reality, each actor in the network has its own beliefs followed by subsequent actions. So, it is unlikely for a state to impose its will on a society when policy networks exist (Pierre, 2000). However, this is not to say that the state has lost the ability to govern but rather that a policy network could be used as a means to restore it (Enroth, 2011). In that sense, we can strongly argue that it is worthwhile to acknowledge the role of the state in the policy networks - being a network of networks.

Despite its anticipated accomplishments, policy networks may not always be beneficial in terms of outcome. The actors may be unclear, and there could be hidden clusters that are not observed but play a major role (Kingdon, 1984). The advocacy coalition framework, which focuses on the belief systems of the subsystems, is inherently exclusive (Sabatier, 1988, 1999). Though the policy network is not as exclusive as the advocacy coalition, it is relatively more exclusive than the issue network (Ko, 2007). Thus, the mere involvement of diverse actors cannot warrant effectiveness. As Goldsmith and Eggers (2004) argued, we need to consider the usefulness and effectiveness of the policy network as well as its process of interaction among the actors.

In sum, analyzing a disaster response system requires both hierarchical and network approaches. COVID-19 is not only a health issue, but also an economic, social, and global issue. To quickly recognize the problem and allocate resources, well-designed command and control systems and various response methods are needed through joint consideration by various organizations. In this regard, the role of the government and civil society in policy networks is important. In policy implementation, the attention put on the policy network does not replace the power of government agencies (McGuire & Bevir, 2011), and the performance of government agencies in implementation is evaluated by effectiveness. Thus, we should not be framed in the policy network as a mere process but assess its contribution to effectiveness in implementation. Such an effort would be complemented by recognizing the hierarchical structure of governmental organizations, which maintains comparatively clear boundaries of actors and their roles within the network.

## 3.2  Rational, Heuristic, and Collaboratory Approaches

Although the structural approach is useful in explaining the overall disaster management system, it is not enough to explain why organizations and decision-makers choose one alternative over the others. As disaster management is inherently a series of decision-makings, many different frameworks focusing on decision-making are proposed in this regard.

### *3.2.1 Rational Approach*

The underlying assumption of rational choice theory is that complex social phenomena can be reduced and explained based on individual actions that comprise society (Scott, 2000). These individuals are considered to have goals that convey their preferences, which are attempted to achieve given certain constraints and with the information they have (Scott, 2000). Rational choice theorists assume that rational actors know what they want to achieve (goal), and the various means through which the goal is achieved. Moreover, rational individuals can determine which goal offers them the highest satisfaction out of the multiple alternatives (Heath, 1976; Carling, 1991; Coleman,

2017). These assumptions are unrealistic in some disaster situations. For instance, while minimizing the infection and fatality seems to be both reasonable goals, it is uncertain that the former should be prioritized if many infected patients are asymptomatic. Similarly, while people believed that a comprehensive COVID-19 test would be desirable, if the costs of the tests far surpass the benefits, the test would not be a desirable means to control COVID-19 (Ko & Hong, 2020). Likewise, the goals may be more important to treat patients than to minimize confirmed cases or fatalities, and mental health is as important as physical health. Additionally, minimizing the economic damage caused by the coronavirus may also be a goal. It is common for various goals to exist, and whether one goal should be prioritized over another is not necessarily a matter of rational judgment, but rather a matter of political judgment. Furthermore, these judgments often vary depending on the decision-maker.

Also, citizens' cognition is not necessarily based on rationality but on social psychology. Indeed, cognition plays a critical role in the performance of emergency management (Comfort, 2007). When referred to as the ability to recognize the risk, the concept of cognition is more or less confined to perceptive aspects. But when further extended to the actions taken on the basis of that recognition - or information - cognition gains more practical value with respect to disaster management. Facing COVID-19, people are unable to adapt to the changing situation and it is not always possible for the various actors to achieve the same level of cognition.

How could a rational approach explain the collective actions of actors in the response system if there is no individual incentive to support such joint efforts? Olson (1965) attributed such support for collective action to 'selective incentives', which modify the rewards and costs so that the collective action is beneficial. And with time, people learn from experience that cooperation promotes mutual advantage though it may not generate the maximum outcome for one individual (Scott, 2000). Even if it may bring loss to them for now, people anticipate it could be traded in for profit later in the future (Blau, 1964). Such a willingness to incur costs at present in exchange for future profit, called 'long-term reciprocity' (Blau, 1964), is one of the explanations for why rational actors might participate in collective efforts despite present costs.

However, the rational approach only provides a limited understanding of how actors within a system take action in an urgent environment. Individuals in the market system do not engage in transactions to maximize the social goods as they do not know how their transactions will affect the market equilibrium. The limited cognitive capacity inhibits individuals from managing complex and uncertain environments. There is also no guarantee that policymakers are armed with better rationality than individuals considering the politically constrained nature of government policymaking. Because of such constraints in cognition, policymakers are only able to focus on limited aspects of a problem and derive a partial selection of possible solutions. Thus, scholars explored alternative approaches to explain heuristic and self-organization processes through social interactions.

### 3.2.2 Heuristic Approach

In arguing that people's rationality in decision-making is limited, some scholars have incorporated concepts such as satisficing, limited cognition, limited search process, etc. (March & Simon, 1958; Nisbett & Ross, 1980; Kahneman et al., 1982). In actual instances, alternatives of solution are examined sequentially, which makes the decision-makers with bounded rationality regard the first "satisficing" alternative that is appropriate to be selected (Simon, 1990). In public policy, time and money allocated for certain policy problems are limited, so public agencies restrict their attention to a few values and alternatives (Lindblom, 1959). Thus, rather than probing all possible alternatives, decision-makers outline the first few alternatives that occurred and compare them.

Unlike rationalists' argument that actions are the outcomes of rational choice which considers possible alternatives, Weick (1988) contends that actions themselves determine situations. He argues that people know what the appropriate action is only after they take action (Weick, 1988). Consequently, one's previous response affects the directions for the following responses, in turn impacting the whole situation. Under dynamic conditions, in particular, when complexity subdues order, actions taken previously may mean much more than they are in normality. The actions taken by the actors build an environment in which subsequent decisions are made. Therefore, it is not assessing the accuracy of the knowledge but screening and interpreting "actionable knowledge" that matters (Bettis & Prahalad, 1995). Weick (1995) used the term "sensemaking" to describe the idea that is driven by plausibility instead of accuracy. However, as Weick and colleagues (2005) have argued, the distribution of information among various actors, each having different impressions about the situation, makes it difficult to harmonize such disparities. Hutchins (1995) referred to "distributed cognition". Such a notion calls for learning how to work collectively with cognitions diversified among the relevant actors. Learning is a rational activity of humans, but this rationality is not something predetermined. Instead, it is a process where information obtained through a continuous process of rationalization is returned to action. In disaster management, most response manuals are not created by predicting the future but are the result of lessons learned from past experiences. The human heuristics approach can also be seen as a result of these rational learning processes rather than completely random behavior.

Heuristics, a decision-making mechanism that relies on partial and readily available information, has been widely utilized in human behavior to facilitate swift and efficient decision-making in the face of uncertainty (Mousavi,

2018). In contrast to the rational approach, which assumes that decision-makers are fully rational and able to process all available information, the heuristic approach acknowledges the complexity of the decision-making environment and considers the rationality of a decision in light of the available information within that environment. Given the ever-changing nature of the disaster context, decision-makers often find themselves unable to consider all potential information, and thus rely on heuristics to derive the best possible decision based on the available information. As such, heuristics provide a valuable means of decision-making in dynamic environments with constantly evolving information.

In early 2020, a debate arose regarding the efficacy of wearing masks in reducing the risk of COVID-19 infection. Public officials in the United States, including infectious disease expert Dr. Anthony Fauci, did not initially encourage Americans to wear masks, as late as March of that year. It was not until the pandemic had escalated that the U.S. Center for Disease Control and Prevention (CDC) began advising the wearing of masks, on April 2, 2020. This hesitation toward mask usage was attributable to both the scarcity of N95 masks and a cultural emphasis on individualism over collectivism (Kemmemmeier & Jami, 2021). Thus, this decision was not based on a rational analysis of the risks, but rather on cultural psychology and political context. Conversely, in Korea, the majority of the population wore masks despite having limited information regarding the extent to which wearing masks could reduce the risk of COVID-19 transmission. The Korean population wore masks not only out of immediate self-interest but also out of a sense of civic duty to protect others in the community. Moreover, compliance with social distancing policies, vaccination, and taking COVID-19 tests was not solely based on rational individual decisions grounded in scientific information.

The heuristics approach is robust in that it ignores some factors that might emanate changes. Within rapidly changing environments where systems are interdependent, it is unlikely that actors take actions based on certainty. Under such conditions, taking action first and then learning retrospectively may be a more plausible approach instead of taking action based on accurate knowledge. Thus, Weick's idea of sensemaking seems to maintain practical value in a world of extreme uncertainty, with its ongoing feedback process.

However, the value of the heuristic approach in disaster response is a double-edged sword. If an individual's risk cognition is too strong, people do not change their behaviors according to newly found scientific evidence. For instance, when people died of COVID-19, the Korean government enforced cremation of the dead body, while WHO argues that the cremation of persons who have died of a communicable disease is simply a matter of cultural choice and available resources, not a mandatory practice (WHO, 2020). Despite the scientific evidence, the Korean government had not changed the mandatory cremation policy until January 2022. The myth that communicable disease infection is still possible through the dead body was making sense to policymakers.

### 3.2.3 Collaboratory Approach

Traditional rationalistic or heuristics approach assumes an individual as the representative actor and their decision behavior would be similar to that of an organization or even a government. But, in reality, many disaster management problems arise and are resolved through the process of interaction between various actors. In this sense, it is necessary to fully understand the collectiveness of the policy.

Collaboration is "any joint activity by two or more agencies that is intended to increase public value by working together rather than separately" (Bardach, 1998). However, because different actors come together, the extent to which actors agree on the common goal may vary. Consequently, this brings variations on what form of collaboration one chooses to obtain the goal.

A pandemic requires a global level of collaboration. Even if most countries successfully prevent the spread of the pandemic such as COVID-19, the failure of disease control in the United States, China, or highly connected countries causes international failure of disease control. Unfortunately, COVID-19 has introduced policies that harm solidarity between countries, such as border closures in each country, export blockage of major medical resources, and monopoly purchase of vaccines, predominantly in developed countries. Consequently, developed countries were able to quickly secure medical resources to respond to COVID-19 and lower the fatality rate, but African countries found themselves in a situation where they could not properly lower the fatality rate over time. Additionally, unlike other countries, China has remained a potential risk country for COVID-19 spread as it pursues a zero COVID policy. The importance of international solidarity is immense, but discussions on international cooperation against the pandemic have not been active during the COVID-19 process. The WHO faced criticism for showing pro-China behavior prior to declaring it a pandemic in March 2020, and U.S. President Trump officially notified the WHO of its withdrawal in July 2020. The weakening of WHO, which was an important international organization that would lead cooperation by coordinating interests between countries, has become a key factor that makes international cooperation difficult. Moreover, the spread of nationalism that emerged through the process of border closure and conflict between the United States and China has become a factor that makes joint quarantine efforts around the world a difficult matter.

Collaboration is an essential framework for comprehending disaster response within a country. Feiock (2013) proposed the Institutional Collective Action (ICA) framework by drawing upon transaction cost theories of contracts. ICA dilemmas arise from the division of authority, whereby decisions made by one government in a specific functional area affect other governments and/or functions. This fragmentation of policy responsibility leads to diseconomies of scale, positive and negative externalities, and common property resources problems. To address these issues, institutions engage in collaboration mechanisms that range from informal networks to various levels of government. The participants in such collaborations are incentivized to select the type of collaboration mechanism that aligns with their cost estimates, wherein transaction costs are the highest when collaboration is mandated by the authority and lowest when it is voluntary. However, transaction costs do not necessarily pertain only to monetary costs, but also encompass noneconomic costs such as psychological costs that arise from the process of social interaction. Furthermore, the behavior of a group can vary depending on which costs are given greater weight. In disaster management situations, cooperation within formal systems is preferred due to the high cost of information search. In particular, voluntary participation and cooperation within the public system can be facilitated if the system is designed to accommodate a range of actors, thus enhancing the effectiveness of disaster response.

In emergency management, collaboration often takes the form of partnership, which involves public, private, and nonprofit sectors and also engaging media, communities, and citizens (Kapucu et al., 2010). Due to the limited time and resources in emergencies, especially in large-scale disasters, understanding and agreement on the common goal from individual participants are challenging. Thus, it is critical to develop and maintain the disaster response system based on shared knowledge, including the common goal, measures, and information about the risk. To achieve this shared knowledge status, administrative principles such as transparency, participation, openness, and flexibility are well embedded within the collaborative governance.

In order to understand how actions are derived from commonly shared knowledge, the next step is to identify the primary decision points within a dynamic inter-organizational system. Comfort (2007) identifies these decision points as the detection of risk, recognition and interpretation of risk, communication of risk, and self-organization and mobilization of a collective, community response system. These decision points expand in context from the epicenter of the risk to the immediate and wider regions, and ultimately to the entire community (Comfort, 2007). Within these decision points, information serves as the foundation for a "common knowledge base" that facilitates collective action to reduce risk (Comfort, 2007). In complex adaptive systems where interaction defines the system (La Porte, 2015), timely and accurate information initiates collective cognition and action throughout the system (Argyris & Schon, 1978; Argyris, 1993). During this process, personal values and social connections influence the transition from knowledge to action (Comfort, 2019). Comfort (2019) argues that individuals are more likely to take action when their immediate family, friends, and community are at risk, thereby transforming individual cognition into collective cognition that guides subsequent actions.

This whole process of linking individual cognition to collective cognition in disaster response is critical both theoretically and practically. No individuals facing extreme events are rational as assumed in a rational approach. Rather, individuals with bounded rationality and higher-level groups constituted of those individuals are subject to making errors contrary to rationalists' beliefs. Subsequently, individuals make decisions based on limited cognition, which would later be shifted into collective cognition. However, because an individual's cognitions are "distributed" (Hutchins, 1995), the conversion from individual to collective cognition becomes a crucial yet difficult task.

In practice, avoiding the disconnect between individual cognition and collective cognition is necessary to maintain the emergency management system which engages multiple governments, agencies, and other associated organizations. In Korea, the COVID-19 pandemic disclosed the discrepancy in information accessibility within groups of people who are not as accustomed to using mobile phones or the internet. One example was buying public masks when the number of cases was soaring and the demand for them reached its peak. The groups who could not acquire real-time information on the pharmacies with enough masks in stock could not buy masks. This surfaced as a serious problem since they were mostly the elderly who were more likely to be vulnerable to the virus. In this regard, the collaboration should include different gender, age, and social classes. Unfortunately, such inclusion of diverse groups into collaborative governance of disaster management is frequently overlooked as many of them did not have well-organized representatives.

The decision-making process for disaster management involves a combination of rational, heuristic, and collaborative approaches, as these frameworks are not mutually exclusive. However, responding to complex disasters such as COVID-19 requires a flexible approach that can adapt to the constantly changing situation. The emphasis on cooperation in existing theories highlights the shared goal of solving the problem, but prioritizing individual freedom versus group safety remains a challenge. Heuristic approaches can be useful, but in some cases, policy decisions must be made without a clear objective basis, leading to decision avoidance. As a result, the decision-making process is constantly evolving, and a combination of rational, heuristic, and collaborative approaches is often necessary. It is essential to recognize that continuous learning is required to select an appropriate decision-making model, rather than asserting the superiority of one approach over another. Therefore, the perspective of policy learning provides a useful framework for understanding the governance framework of disaster management.

## 3.3 Policy Learning within Dynamic Environment

Rational, heuristic, and collective action approaches are appropriate to understanding the decision-making and behavior patterns of individuals or groups. However, policies tend to emerge in the confines of policy arena, which are narrower than the social space where deterministic social interactions occur. Such policy venues can be participated in by all members of society, but it tends to incur a lot of time and cost. Therefore, those who can participate in policymaking are often limited to key actors. Policy network is a structure that focuses on the interaction between key actors or organizations in the policy arena.

Policy actors in disaster management systems work within both hierarchies of government and form policy networks in which they employ rational, heuristic, and collaborative approaches to understand and solve imminent problems. Their experiences, in turn, become another factor choosing the future direction of their responses. Policy-learning framework assumes that planning is doomed to be incomplete and implementation gap between the plan and actual policy is far wider than we expect (Pressman & Wildavsky, 1984). An ever-changing environment requires a new problem definition, and an incomplete plan requires continuous policy revision at the implementation stage (Wildavsky, 1979). It is important to understand disaster response as a policy-learning process. If information and experience gained during the disaster response are not learned and shared by numerous policy actors, new problems that emerged during the spread of disasters or wrong errors in past responses can be corrected.

### 3.3.1 Cognition as a Necessary Condition of Learning

The initial step toward learning is identifying what needs to be changed or overcome. However, mere identification of the problem is insufficient for achieving learning. According to Crossan et al. (1995), integrative learning occurs only when cognitive and behavioral changes take place. This idea aligns with the notion that cognition plays a critical role in activating the response activities of multiple actors (Comfort, 2007). Similarly, Klein (1993) emphasized the significance of cognition in decision-making, particularly for leaders who are faced with unpredictable problems. These perspectives underscore the importance of not only recognizing the problem but also taking action within the environment in which it is situated. Human cognition frequently drives behavior, rather than rational analysis and judgment, leading to immediate actions based on perception before a rational decision is made.

Given the rapidly changing environment, prompt actions are essential, and the dissemination of information from individuals to the broader community is crucial. Shared information and knowledge can impact risk cognition, just as it is used for rational analysis and judgment. However, the degree to which shared information and knowledge changes individual or societal risk cognition varies. For instance, during the COVID-19 pandemic, an abundance of knowledge and information was disseminated globally, but the level of risk perception varied from country to country. In this regard, policy should intervene to facilitate response activities by connecting individual cognition to collective action. Nevertheless, the intricate policy network structure, characterized by interdependence, presents an even more challenging role for the government in the face of emerging risks. The disaster management system comprises different levels of government, emergency personnel, public, private, and nonprofit organizations. Therefore, governments must swiftly distribute information and interpret it to derive timely and appropriate actions. Due to the rapid development of information and communication technologies, the COVID-19 response has led to faster sharing of crisis awareness among citizens compared to past disaster responses. Even countries with low sensitivity to crises are now able to obtain real-time information about the COVID-19 situation, which is spreading rapidly in other countries. They are also able to access information about various policies being adopted by different countries and their effectiveness. This sharing of crisis awareness means that individuals, communities, countries, and the world as a whole can benefit from it.

According to Comfort (2019), personal values and social connections promote shifting knowledge to action. Therefore, when one's immediate family, friends, and community are faced with risk, people tend to take action (Comfort, 2019). This idea provides implications for the policymakers who ought to minimize the disconnection of cognition between the individual and the wider community at risk. In striving for methods to enhance emergency response, policymakers should be able to link one individual to another in cognitive chains and ultimately empower the community to be adaptive to disaster. As such, cognition, assumed to be followed by action, serves as a necessary condition upon which learning takes place.

### 3.3.2  Learning in the Process of Adapting to the Dynamic Environment

Adding to the inherent complexity in policy networks due to interdependency and pluralism, the dynamic environments by which the disasters are affected contribute to even larger complexities. In disaster management, much like many other systems that involve multiple organizations, the engagement of diverse actors itself comprises a complex system. Such a system is conceptualized as a 'complex adaptive system' where 'agents' influence one another and alter the environment through their actions. The major features of a complex adaptive system are that agents are heterogeneous, and they are able to adapt their behavior on the basis of their interactions with other agents, as the interaction produces the nonlinearity and unexpected outcomes. Due to the process, the new behaviors and patterns emerge through interactions and adaptive efforts of agents. The diverse agents' performance depends on others and the system, which impacts the agent back again through the feedback loop (Chiva-Gómez, 2003). In a way, the components that are impacted by the dynamic environment become an environment themselves.

Because organizations themselves are deemed a complex adaptive system (Anderson, 1999; Axelrod & Cohen, 1999; Gell-Mann, 1994), they maintain their capacity by constant learning, which allows them to be adaptive to the shifting conditions. As such, organizational learning or interorganizational learning takes place in every complex adaptive system and the actors strive for survival. However, unlike in normality, extreme conditions inhibit the actors from conducting holistic assessments about themselves and others since the environment is changing continuously and the time is short. In such a situation where knowledge is limited and uncertainty is high, the diversity of situations created by a changing complex adaptive system does not explode into disorder because of the adaptability of the system that creates a self-organizing state. This self-organizing state does not necessarily mean a desirable state, but rather a state with high adaptability to the given environment. In order for high adaptability to be possible, continuous learning and various attempts to adapt to the environment must be made through the operation of the law of survival of the fittest. For this reason, learning in a complex adaptive system is not mechanical repetitive learning, but proactive and adaptive activities to increase adaptability. Therefore, self-organization is not achieved through the results of inexplicable random behavior, but rather by conscious activities aimed at adaptation and survival in the interaction with the environment, not just within the system.

The policy network within a complex system preserves both stability and change. Baumgartner and Jones (1993) conceptualized policy stability and change, which can be applied to policy networks affected by external shocks. According to their notion of punctuated equilibrium, long periods of stability are interrupted by occasional large events that break the stability and lead to dramatic policy change. In disaster settings, unexpected events can disturb the stability of policies, prompting changes to adapt to the new environment. For example, the 9/11 terrorist attack in the United States resulted in a change in government organizations with the creation of the Department of Homeland Security. Prior to this event, institutional checks and balances had made it difficult for the president to restructure the government.

As seen from the dynamic environment in which the actors struggle to adapt to and survive, observing and analyzing what is learned and how is so important in maintaining organizations' capacity amidst disaster. Moreover, the extreme conditions set forth by the disaster provide opportunity for the policy networks to change, which allows the system as a whole to change by implementing lessons learned.

Learning could take place during the crisis, but it comes with high consequentiality, limited time, high political salience, uncertainty, and ambiguity (Moynihan, 2008). And thus, such constraints hamper actors from achieving appropriate responses. On the other hand, some argue that the experiences gained from the actual crises create the ability to handle the time pressure and acknowledge the need to change the rule (Comfort et al., 1989; Lagadec, 1990). Moreover, Ko (2020) assumes that the innate barrier of crisis learning associated with networks and complex adaptive systems is likely to improve learning within networks. The learning from the crisis is further discussed with respect to effectiveness of response providing implications for the response management (Ko, 2020).

The heuristics approach is likely to be activated during the crisis with its characteristics of making fast and frugal decisions. In this case, actions already taken serve as a basis on which subsequent actions are taken (Weick, 1988). Thus, the role of the government entities during disaster, particularly of those who take a significant role in decision-making, is to seek ways to coordinate actions by various actors within the policy network. This requires the government to learn from short-term experience, while the situation is still evolving.

Learning during a crisis is learning all the while managing the imminent situations, so the role of the government to connect and coordinate dispersed cognitions and actions becomes even more complicated. In a way, this relies on how those memories stored by actors are connected to the group level, and all the way up to the network level. With the networks of organizations interlinked, it is the *transactive memory* among multiple actors creating a set of shared knowledge (Wegner, 1995). This aligns with how disaster response involves the process of cognition, communication, coordination, and control (Comfort, 2007). Therefore, by utilizing the shared knowledge generated by actors of the network, learning is made possible even while uncertainty is prevailing.

### 3.3.3 Outcomes of Learning Embedded in Institutions and Value System: Explicit and Implicit Learning

Learning is a measurement of success in crisis response (Moynihan, 2008), and a network itself is viewed as a "learning system" because the generation of valid information, informed choice, and timely commitment to action largely impact the crisis response network (Comfort, 1988). The governments and the major actors in the network are continuously being evaluated by what they have managed to achieve. Such assessments are not merely confined to a single crisis, but lingers until the next one. Therefore, the governments, especially the public managers in the disaster management field, are bound by the constant urge for implementing lessons learned from previous experiences.

In the case of Korea, MERS in 2015 served as a prehistory from which implementations in COVID-19 could seek reference from. Though the scale and characteristics of the two are disparate, the basic operational frameworks in disaster management could be shared. Ko (2020) argued that the Korean government's response to COVID-19 was effective with respect to the nature of the network task along with its hierarchical bureaucracy. This was ascribed to the policy learning from MERS, which contributed to accelerated response activities.

As discussed earlier, organizations as complex adaptive systems innately possess learning mechanisms. This means that learning is a driving force of facilitating the systems to maintain their status through constant feedback. In order for a system to survive, it should be capable of deriving lessons from the past and implement it to current situations. The complex adaptive systems' learning mechanism incorporates not only single-loop learning but also double-loop learning. According to Argyris (1991), while single-loop learning attempts to solve the problem based on set goals and decision-making rules, double-loop learning acknowledges the way a problem is defined and solved, and thus modifies its goals and decision-making rules that govern the problem. In practice, particularly in dynamic settings of disaster, executing change on underlying policies and assumptions is a critical part of management. This highlights the importance of double-loop learning within the complex adaptive system which strengthens the connection between the feedback and mental models of the organizations.

Admitting the fact that organizations, as well as individuals, learn, we may think of two types of learning based on how collective memory is stored and applied: explicit and implicit learning. Explicit learning is observed in formal institutions such as organizational structure, standard operating procedures (SOPs), laws etc. El Sawy and colleagues (1986) view organizations as collectives of individuals, which makes it possible that *institutional memory* is stored and retrieved (Corbett et al., 2020). Without memory being stored, the knowledge gained from learning might easily fade away when the participants exit and accessibility of record becomes difficult (El Sawy et al., 1986). Institutional memory can be of different types, such as formal, informal, tacit, and digital institutional. The reason that individuals' or organizations' learning does not disappear but is internalized in the organization is that it is transformed into institutionalized memory with a variety of forms. Therefore, information management is stressed with its capacity to capture how organizational participants gain understanding about the past and the present, which shapes the future (El Sawy et al., 1986). Rather than being a passive actor in creating and running institutional memory, organizations act as interpretation systems by incorporating patterns or processes through which meaning is created and shared (Daft & Weick, 1984). Standard operating procedure is an example of memory being stored explicitly, reflecting what has been learned from the past and is codified into rules of action (El Sawy et al., 1986).

Seen from the policymaking process perspective, learning is derived from the constant process where an aggregate of information is linked to policy implementation and performance (Linder & Peters, 1990). The learning based on knowledge and information formulates policy, which is followed by policy performance and implementation (Linder & Peters, 1990). In Linder and Peters' (1990) terminology, the *guidance mechanism* is a means of institutionalizing learning so that it could be adapted into policy processes. Once inferences from the past are embedded in the routines, such institutions define what will be considered error, thus need correction. This closely aligns with the double-loop learning (Argyris, 1991) in that the norms and rules for judgments could be corrected through accumulations of experiences. As diverse as it may be, the outcomes of learning could be addressed in explicit forms and convey meaningful information and knowledge gained from experiences. Learning may also be ingrained implicitly in the value systems of people. Though this kind of learning may be less vivid than institutionalized forms of learning, it contains significant impact because once a value system is deeply rooted in people's lives, it lasts until other compelling efforts to transform that system are in effect. Shaw and Perkins (1992) claimed that belief systems generate outcomes through actions and the outcomes are reflected and brought insight, which in turn affects the very belief system creating the constant rounds of feedback. In such an aspect, it goes hand in hand with explicit learning in that people's perceptions, belief systems, and values shape institutions, which shapes them back again (Linder & Peters, 1990).

*Schema* is defined as "a set of rules based on experience of a cognitive structure which induces action" (Anderson, 1999; Stacey, 1996). In organizations, schema can be presented as routines as a result of interactive patterns of interaction (Axelrod & Cohen, 1999). Levitt and March (1988) also consider routines as being results of "recurrent sequences of action" encompassing multiple organizational actors. Just as individuals make use of schema to act, organizations apply their routines to act upon occurrences. Because learning encoded in routines is maintained despite extensive turnover of rule makers and rule users (Schulz, 2017), it keeps stability under hierarchical approach. However, as we have discussed so far, the learning mechanism inherent in complex adaptive systems provides grounds on which those routines are transformed when external stimuli compel them to change. This is especially observable in disasters where the emergent situations serve as *exogenous shocks* changing the rules which were once thought stable. Whereas explicit learning contributes to developing the hardware, implicit learning operates as the software, permeating into the individuals, organizations, and the communities. In other words, these two types of learning are not exclusive of, but are complementary to each other.

## 3.4 Conceptual Framework

Figure 3.1 illustrates the conceptual framework based on the discussions so far incorporating multiple approaches to analyze response systems in pandemics. Our conceptual model emphasizes the holistic approach to disaster management that includes a structural perspective, a decision-making perspective, a complex adaptive systems perspective, and a policy-learning perspective. Of course, not all actors participating in disaster management adopt a comprehensive approach. Sometimes the focus is on the structural perspective, and sometimes the complex adaptive systems perspective is adopted. In the early stages of a disaster, for instance, because uncertainty is high, response begins under the governance system formed according to established laws and

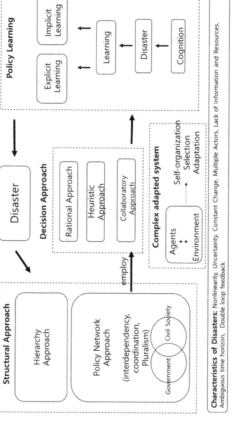

*Figure 3.1* Conceptual framework. Characteristics of disasters: nonlinearity, uncertainty, constant change, multiple actors, lack of information and resources, ambiguous time horizon, and double-loop feedback.

response manuals before the disaster occurs. However, as each actor's diverse response experience accumulates to address various unexpected problems, a new governance structure is formed. From the perspective of complex adaptive systems or policy networks, a process of addressing and solving problems through continuous interaction among actors leads to jointly developing new disaster response strategies. In this process, the government's role seems to be absolutely crucial, but in reality, innovation in private enterprise, cooperation between civil society and government, cooperation between central and local governments, and solidarity of the international community, all contribute significantly to the effectiveness of disaster response. Of course, this process of interaction does not always appear in the form of cooperation. Sometimes conflict and competition arise in the process of pursuing different objectives. It is impossible for the central government to coordinate all such complex interactions. The uncertainty caused by a disaster situation is so great, and finding the optimal response method is so difficult that political rationality rather than instrumental rationality becomes more important in making rational decisions. This inevitably leads to the emergence of policy learning as a key element in the disaster management model, making flexible disaster response strategies possible. Such policy learning occurs not only in individuals' learning but also in the entire disaster management system, becoming a core element that leads to changes in subsequent laws, governance structures, policy networks, and cooperation networks.

From the perspective of actors, a holistic approach is very obvious. It is not possible to secure citizen compliance with various social distancing policies or the recognition of risks associated with infectious diseases like COVID-19 through the strong leadership of a few rational policymakers or specific departments. Innumerable new ideas are generated through the everyday activities of numerous actors, and innovations in disaster response are achieved through an inclusive approach. To incorporate various actors into the disaster response network, a new capability beyond managing ministries or public organizations is required of the government. The applicability of the holistic approach is heightened by the democratic system, which inherently incorporates respect for various actors, competition and cooperation among different stakeholders, and experiences with uncertainty. In particular, democratic countries with high levels of autonomy in civil society may not be able to respond effectively in the short term due to the uncertainty associated with disasters, but their flexible system allows them to adapt quickly to disaster situations and to improve the social system through policy learning after the disaster. If disaster response is carried out by a few powerful individuals or organizations, the effectiveness of the response may temporarily appear to be high, but there is a greater likelihood that capacity will deteriorate when facing various disasters that may arise in the future. This is because learning by a few is difficult to internalize in the social system as a whole.

While operations of the response system will be scrutinized in terms of participants' actions within the policy network, the underlying assumption is that cognition stimulates subsequent actions of the participants. This idea is based on Simon's (1982) notion about an individual's limited cognitive capacity and Comfort's (2007) idea of viewing cognition as a critical component of response activities. In crises, policy networks composed of participants with individual cognition necessitate collective cognition in order to cope with the increasing demand for a timely response. The policymakers and public managers in the field are responsible for minimizing the disconnection between individual cognition and collective cognition to enhance the response system as a whole.

Learning takes place both during and after a crisis. While the crisis situation is still elevating, response activities require much effort, but the extreme uncertainty also yields opportunities to learn and adapt to changing environments. When the crisis is over, the policy network as a learning system recognizes, retrospectively, what has been done well and what has not. Such a retrospective approach assesses the outcomes of responses to a crisis. Assuming that prior experiences affect future responses, this sort of learning impacts subsequent crises in explicit and implicit forms. Explicitly, changes are applied in institutions, formalized laws and rules, and so on. Implicitly, learning is implemented in the value system of the policy network and ultimately of the wider community.

Framing a response system, particularly in an unprecedented crisis like COVID-19, is a challenging task. This is partly due to extremely rapid changes in the environments which makes it demanding to achieve established goals, and partly due to the system itself, which consists of divergent actors interdependent on one another. Yet, the participants of the policy network contribute to developing better response systems by operating learning mechanisms inherent in their own complex adaptive systems. Such an ongoing feedback process from cognition to action, to learning, and then back to cognition via explicit and implicit forms of learning delineates how double-loop learning adjusts the goals and decision-making rules. It implies the possibility of improving the system by reflecting on past experiences to be applied for future implementations. This framework, derived from literature on structural approach, cognitive approach, and learning in complexity, will serve as a lens through which the aim of this book demonstrating how the Korean government managed to achieve an effective response to the pandemic without imposing authoritative measures is attained.

## Note

1 The Sewol ferry sank on the morning of April 16, 2014, caused 306 deaths out of 476 passengers. The poor response to the disaster was one of reasons that President Park Geun-Hye was impeached in 2017.

# 4 Learning from the MERS Experience in Korea

The capacity of disaster response has proven to be closely related to the degree of preparedness, which includes measures such as the legal system clarifying the chain of command and mobilization of the public resources, development of manuals for multiagency coordination and standard operation procedure, proper maintenance and training of response organizations, and securing the requisite supplies and equipment. Although many scholars claim that the MERS crisis in 2015 was a primary factor in Korea's successful response (Ko, 2020), these preparedness measures have developed through intentional efforts for a long time even before the MERS crisis.

Severe Acute Respiratory Syndrome (SARS) started in 2003 in China. It then spread to Hong Kong, Singapore, Vietnam, and North America, horrifying many countries due to the high contagions and fatality. Interestingly, the Korean government on March 16, 2003, even brought in military medical staff for the control of communicable diseases at their airports and other entry points, right after noticing that China had a suspicious pneumonia case. Citizens were unaccustomed to such intensive communicable disease control, and many complained that the government overreacted. However, there was zero infection and no fatal cases in Korea, which enabled the Koreans to realize the importance of quick response to epidemics.

The Korean government established an agency for taking care of epidemics under the unified authority from the SARS response experience. During the SARS crisis, the point-of-entry screening and the quarantine function were not well coordinated as different agencies managed two functions. The information-sharing among agencies did not work due to the barrier of bureaucratic red tape and the organizational silo effect. Responding to the criticism, the Korean government enhanced its institutional capacity by establishing the Korea Center for Disease Control and Prevention (KCDC) to integrate research, border screening, and quarantine of diseases and epidemics in 2004.

The Korean government also changed the legal structure and created a new organization. During the MERS crisis in 2015, the Korean government did not disclose the hospital name where a patient was hospitalized and did not share the information with other organizations because of privacy. The hospitals did not share patients' information promptly with the government, and there

DOI: 10.4324/9781003125006-4

was no system for the voluntary reports of suspicious patients. Moreover, the tracking system of a patient and his/her contacts were not well-established. Consequently, one super-spreader infected almost 90 people. Of course, there was a justification for not disclosing the hospital's name. As Korea has a stringent privacy protection law and private information is only sharable under strict conditions, keeping the infected patients' hospital names private was considered to protect patients' privacy and hospitals. To resolve the problem, the Korean government revised the Infectious Disease Control and Prevention Act (IDCPA) in 2015, allowing the government to introduce standard operating procedures for tracking patients. Following the revision of the IDCPA, the Korean government can legally track confirmed patients' contacts and places they visited during the COVID-19 crisis in 2020 without serious debate over privacy issues.

SARS and MERS experiences still did not resolve the issue of communication and collaboration. In the MERS crisis, hospitals, medical experts, and local governments played significant roles in detecting and treating patients, but their authorities and channels to participate in policymaking were ambiguous. They were not sure who the command center was. The Presidential office, the Prime Minister's office, the Minister of Public Health and Welfare, and the commissioner of the KCDC chaired the different disaster response committees at different levels. The KCDC could not exert leadership in such a situation because it was reluctant to take political responsibility. In response to the concern, Korea revised the IDCAP again in 2018 to resolve the confusion in the command center. The 2018 revision of the IDCAP made clear that the KCDC is a command center during the disaster response to infectious diseases.

Lessons drawn from the MERS experience prompted the Korean government to formulate a crisis management governance as shown in Figure 4.1. What is noteworthy about this governance is the division of roles between the Central Disaster Management Headquarters and the Central Disease Control Headquarters. In general, in the case of infectious diseases, it is natural for the KCDC to function as a key response agency. Therefore, when the severity of an infectious disease is low, the Central Disease Control Headquarters (CHCH) was established under the responsibility of KCDC to respond to infectious diseases. However, when the infectious disease reached a serious stage of Level 3 or higher, the Central Disaster Management Headquarters (CDMH) was established under the responsibility of the Minister of Health and Welfare because KCDC lacked the authority and resources to lead other government ministries. However, since the Central Disaster Management Headquarters is not strong enough to coordinate government-wide policies, the command center for disaster response was assigned to the Central Disaster and Safety Countermeasure Headquarters (CDSCH).

CDSCH was headed by the Minister of the Interior and Safety. However, as the seriousness of COVID-19 was recognized, the Prime Minister took

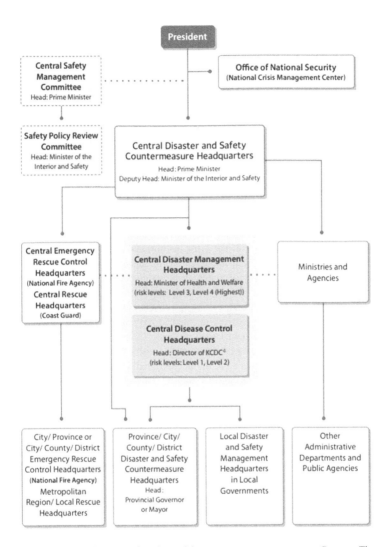

*Figure 4.1* Korea's comprehensive crisis management governance. *Source:* The Government of the Republic of Korea, "All About Korea's Response to COVID-19', 2020, p.33.

responsibility in February 2020, and the Minister of Interior and Safety took charge as the deputy head. With CDSCH at the center, CDCH and CDMH were to play the role of key organizations in responding to infectious diseases, and a governance structure was created for government departments and local governments to interact with this core organization. Rapid response can be possible by clarifying the governance structure and command center related to disaster response before a disaster occurs. At the time of MERS, it was criticized for not having a proper governance structure and policy coordination not working properly.

The response manuals were also developed and revised during MERS responses. The early version of the COVID-19 response manual was concise (24 pages) mainly in reference to the MERS response manual. However, the latest manual (version 9.4 in December 2020) is 230 pages long and offers more accurate information and specific guidelines. The manual clarified each actor's response direction and reduced the coordination costs by clearing the uncertainty of responsibilities and setting standard operating procedures.

An important factor to consider is the institutional memory present within the KCDC. This memory encompasses the organization's response to the MERS outbreak, which was documented in various reports and manuals, as well as in the memories of those who were involved in the response efforts. Following the 2015 MERS outbreak, the government took punitive measures against KCDC officials who were deemed to have failed in their response efforts. Specifically, the Korea Board of Audit ordered disciplinary action against 16 officials, including two from the Ministry of Health and Welfare, 12 from the KCDC, and two from the health department, based on the audit results of "MERS Prevention and Response". One of the officials who was subject to disciplinary action was Dr. Jeong Eun-kyung. However, with the appointment of a new government in 2017, Dr. Jeong Eun-kyung was subsequently named as the head of the KCDC, drawing on her prior experience in responding to the MERS outbreak. As head of the KCDC in 2020, Dr. Jeong Eun-kyung actively responded to the COVID-19 crisis. Had many of the officials with experience in responding to the MERS outbreak left the organization due to disciplinary action, the KCDC's institutional memory of the MERS response may have been significantly weakened.

The learning from the MERS experiences also remains among external experts. The Korean Society of Infectious Diseases, through their response to the MERS outbreak, has published a MERS chronicle after the end of the MERS outbreak in 2017. This MERS chronicle presents a deep analysis of the reasons why the initial response to the MERS failed, analyzing the reasons why group infections in hospitals were not properly controlled. In particular, the absence of information control on the initial movement of patients and the absence of thorough epidemiological investigations were emphasized as important causes of the spread. Additionally, the guidelines related to close contacts were based on inaccurate information, which resulted in the use of loose standards, resulting in regret that they could not prevent the spread. These analysis results are shared among hospitals and medical staff. As a result, the medical experts called for adopting a proactive policy of releasing information on confirmed cases and close contacts in the early stages of Korea's response to the COVID-19 pandemic.

Learning is not always positive. After the MERS outbreak, officials from the KCDC received disciplinary action for not properly responding to the initial cluster infection problem in a timely manner. The responsibility of officials can be divided into passive response and active response. Active response refers to cases where officials exercise discretion beyond what the law requires, which can result in unintended consequences. Although the law does not specify this, it applies to cases where the person in charge promptly isolates patients and discloses information about them. After a disaster ends, many officials are held responsible for this proactive response due to the infringement of personal freedom.

On the other hand, passive responsibility refers to situations where public officials do not take any discretionary action beyond the legal limits even when such actions could be necessary to address the crisis effectively. In such cases, officials act within their legal authority but fail to exercise their discretion, resulting in suboptimal responses and reduced effectiveness in managing the crisis. While such actions are legal, they could still be subject to internal disciplinary actions for failing to act proactively to address the crisis.

The problem is that since the mass disciplinary action after MERS, a bureaucratic culture has developed where officials passively respond to avoid responsibility. As long as the scope of officials' immunity is not clearly defined, officials who have learned that there is a possibility of disciplinary action after infectious disease outbreaks may exhibit behavior that avoids any slight risk of disciplinary action, even if it means avoiding proactive response within the limits of their authorized actions. In fact, the continued demand for PCR testing regulations even in 2022, when the need for COVID-19 testing of overseas travelers decreased, demonstrates the conservative culture of the disease control agency. The delay in lifting the regulations on PCR testing for airport arrivals and wearing masks indoors and outdoors, in comparison to other countries, can also be attributed to the attitude of public officials who were afraid of taking responsibility for the potential relaxation of epidemic prevention measures. Due to the fear of punishment for actions not specified in the official documents, on-site epidemic prevention workers constantly demanded guidelines and manuals on how to respond to the situation. In urgent situations such as infectious disease control, where flexibility is crucial, document-centered bureaucracy remains a powerful organizational principle. This may be because frontline bureaucrats have learned from past experiences that they bear the responsibility for response failure after the disaster is over.

# 5 Analysis of Korea's COVID-19 Responses

## 5.1 Actors in Policy Network

### 5.1.1 Overview

Responding to infectious diseases is not something the government alone can do. Korea was interested in controlling domestic infectious diseases such as tuberculosis, measles, and cholera until severe acute respiratory syndrome (SARS) spread worldwide in 2002. Responses to these infectious diseases were led by the government, especially by the central government. In 2002, the Korean government quickly strengthened airport quarantine, and there were no cases of SARS infections. However, unlike these successful response experiences, the Middle East respiratory syndrome (MERS) spread rapidly in 2015. The key reason for this spread was the outbreak of group infections centered on hospitals. At that time, the government realized the importance of close cooperation with the medical community and began to actively invite medical experts to its task force to listen to their opinions. Additionally, in the process of responding to infectious diseases, the need for laws and systems to coordinate policies among various government organizations, such as the Office of the Prime Minister, the Ministry of Public Administration and Security, the Ministry of Health and Welfare, and the Blue House, can be comprehended.

These lessons from MERS significantly affected the Korean government's response to COVID-19 in 2020. Quick surveillance was made during the first stage of COVID-19. Korea was highly alerted by the progress of COVID-19 in China. Since January 3, 2020, the Korean health authority had started to strengthen surveillance for pneumonia cases in health facilities nationwide. On January 3, the KCDC initiated strengthening public health entry screening through individual temperature checks and health questionnaires from the direct flights from Wuhan to Incheon Airport.[1] Moreover, the KCDC established the "Special Task Force of Unknown Wuhan Pneumonia" (Wuhan City Pneumonia Response Team of Unknown Cause). On January 4, KCDC provided a guideline for Wuhan pneumonia responses and the Korean government shared information about Wuhan travelers with hospitals. Consequently, one hospital reported to the KCDC of a patient who had coughing and soaring

DOI: 10.4324/9781003125006-5

throat symptoms on January 7 as the hospital found that the patient had visited Wuhan.[2] Hospitals were able to quickly identify if the patient had visited Wuhan, because the government shared information on the patient's visit history to Wuhan in the system used by doctors to prescribe a medication called drug use review (DUR). In Korea, doctors can use the DUR system to check if a patient has received medication from other hospitals to prevent medication abuse and side effects, so it was possible. In addition, there were active discussions about the danger of pneumonia caused by Wuhan in online communities of doctors and the Korean Infectious Diseases Society. Doctors' awareness of the medical risk led to active reporting of suspected patients.

The KCDC also shared the authority to test COVID-19 with the City Health and Environment Research Institute of seven provinces to expedite the test on January 16.[3] To prevent errors in test results, the KCDC prohibited local governments and general hospitals from conducting infectious disease tests. However, with the need to quickly determine the presence of infection, permission was granted to public and private medical facilities with qualifications to perform the tests. Considering the nature of bureaucracy that seeks to monopolize authority, it is notable that the rapid test authorization was shared. This quick response was due to the recognition of the importance of early response learned during the MERS outbreak. In fact, the director of the KCDC, Jeong Eun-Kyung, learned the importance of flexible and quick responses at the early stage from her experience of the MERS outbreak.

Such an early risk cognition of COVID-19 can be one of the success factors of Korea's effective response. The KCDC began to develop analysis and test methods for COVID-19 on January 13.[4] It announced that it would develop a new test method within a month. Private medical companies such as Seegene also started to develop the test kits on January 21. Once the test kit was developed, the KCDC issued the emergency use authorization on February 12 within a week after the application for the approval of Seegene. Due to the development of test kits, Korea could reduce the time for testing infection from 24 to 6 hours.

Controversies arose when the KCDC reported the first confirmed patient, a Chinese national traveler who resided in Wuhan on January 20. Many citizens, as well as opposition parties, called for banning travelers from China and intensive preventive measures. The KCDC scaled up the national alert level from Blue (level 1) to Yellow (level 2) but did not adopt the travel ban policy following the WHO recommendation on January 23. Instead, the Ministry of Foreign Affairs increased the level of travel alert to level 2 and asked for high caution for traveling to Wuhan. It was almost two weeks later (February 4) that the Korean government announced the entry ban of travelers from Wuhan, not all Chinese (Figure 5.1).

However, the second outbreak of COVID-19 started on February 19, 2020, due to the Shincheonji (religious cult group) community infection in Daegu City. The Korean government raised its national alert level to the highest level

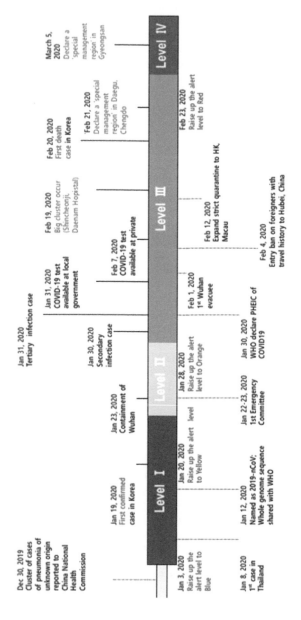

*Figure 5.1* Evolution of COVID-19 in Korea. *Source:* The Republic of Korea (March 31, 2020), "Tackling COVID-19: Health, Quarantine and Economic Measures of South Korea".

(level 4) on February 23 and tested all religious groups in Daegu city. Due to the quick development of test kits, the Korean government could test more than 10,000 suspects every day and continuously increased the number up to 18,000 in early March 2020. At the same time, the Korean government and the civil society began to coordinate limited medical resources. While the national health insurance program provides full accessibility of people to medical services regardless of income, the local government did not have enough medical staff and hospital beds. To respond to such challenges, other local governments less affected by COVID-19 took patients from Daegu. Also, hundreds of doctors and nurses volunteered to take care of patients in Daegu. Moreover, private companies and hospitals provide their facilities as special units for taking light-symptom patients.

Since the development of vaccines in late 2020, Korea made efforts to secure vaccines, but it was not easy because a few countries already bought the most produced vaccines. As a result, the vaccination began in late February 2021, which is late compared to other OECD countries. Despite the delayed vaccine rollout, rapid vaccination of the elderly and high-risk groups was carried out. There have been almost no reports of people illegally getting vaccinated by ignoring the vaccination order. Vaccinations proceeded in accordance with the predetermined order, and the vaccination results were all managed through computerization. In addition, vaccination certification documents were issued to vaccine recipients through a mobile phone app. Vaccinations were mainly conducted in public and private hospitals, with large-scale vaccination facilities installed in public facilities. The selection, notification, and management of vaccine recipients and adverse reactions were quickly provided to citizens through a computerized system. Statistics on COVID-19 vaccine side effects were transparently disclosed to quickly block fake news.

As the Omicron variant spread from the end of 2021, the number of confirmed cases surged, but overloading of medical facilities was prevented through prompt supply of hospital beds. Despite a rapid increase in the number of confirmed cases in February 2022, the fatality rate remained below 0.2%, and the government began to make decisions to ease social distancing policies. This was because the increase in critically ill patients was not significant, and there were enough available hospital beds. Some in the medical community argued against easing social distancing measures, but the government made the decision. Fortunately, the number of confirmed cases began to decrease after April, and social distancing measures began to be relaxed overall from May 2022.

### 5.1.2 *Central Government*

"Who is in charge?" is the key question for understanding how public organizations are aligned in the response system. In the market, no one orders what to buy or how to set a price. In the disaster response system, however, we cannot have enough time and mechanisms to wait for such self-organized equilibrium through voluntary participation. Moreover, the transaction and interaction within the disaster response system happen within hierarchical governance as most key actors of the governance of the response system are bureaucrats and military or police personnel who are too accustomed to command and control culture. Therefore, the organizational chart or the manual indicating the structure of responsibility and authority is very important in resolving conflicts or making decisions.

Who should be in charge? Some argue that experts should be at the center of the response system because they have more knowledge of the technical issues behind COVID-19. For instance, doctors and nurses know better how hospitals work and how the infection test goes on. On the contrary, others argue that bureaucrats should control the governance of the response system for they have better skills on how to manage organizations and policies. Besides, bureaucrats know how to mobilize other civil servants and budgets, and cope with the maze of legal frameworks.

The Korean government makes clear that the KCDC is a responsibility center for disease control. As shown in Figure 5.2, KCDC is not merely an administrative agency for disease control but also performs research. The KCDC operates within the Ministry of Health and Welfare as a line agency.

After raising the country's infectious disease alert level to "highest" (February 23, 2020), the Korean government created the Central Disaster and Safety Countermeasure Headquarters (CDSCHQ), headed by the prime minister, to bolster government-wide responses to COVID-19.

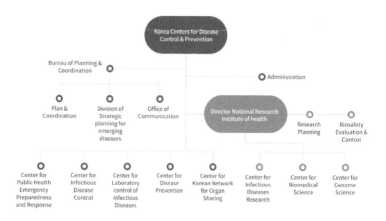

*Figure 5.2* Organizational structure of KCDC. *Source:* KCDC (2020).

Given the distinct nature and expertise involved in responding to an infectious disease, the Central Disease Control Headquarters (KCDC) serves as the command center to prevent and control infection, while the Vice Head 1 of the CDSCHQ, who also serves as the Head of the Central Disaster Management Headquarters (Minister of Health and Welfare), assists in infection prevention and control efforts of the Central Disease Control Headquarters (Head: Director Jeong Eunkyeong of the Korea Centers for Disease Control and Prevention (KCDC)).

The Minister of the Interior and Safety, head of the Pan-government Countermeasures Support Headquarters, assumes the Vice Head 2 will provide necessary assistance such as coordination between the central and the local governments.

At the local government level, the Local Disaster and Safety Countermeasure Headquarters can be established and the heads of the local governments take leadership to manage the headquarters. When the local governments face the surpassing demands beyond their capacity, they can request the central government for providing resources, including beds, human resources, and supplies (Figure 5.3).

As shown in Figure 5.4, the central government has made various efforts, such as strengthening quarantine measures for incoming travelers, quickly identifying confirmed cases, quickly isolating confirmed cases and analyzing their movement paths, securing and distributing various disinfection materials, and securing medical personnel and facilities.

The central government has to mitigate the economic and social impacts of COVID-19. The Korean government has spent a significant amount of money in response to COVID-19 in 2020. According to the Korean government's 2020 supplementary budget plan, a total of 14.3 trillion Korean won (approximately US$12 billion at the time) was allocated for COVID-19 response measures. The main purposes of the budget were to support the health care system, provide economic relief for households and businesses, and strengthen quarantine and prevention measures.

*Figure 5.3* Korean government's response system (as of February 25, 2020).

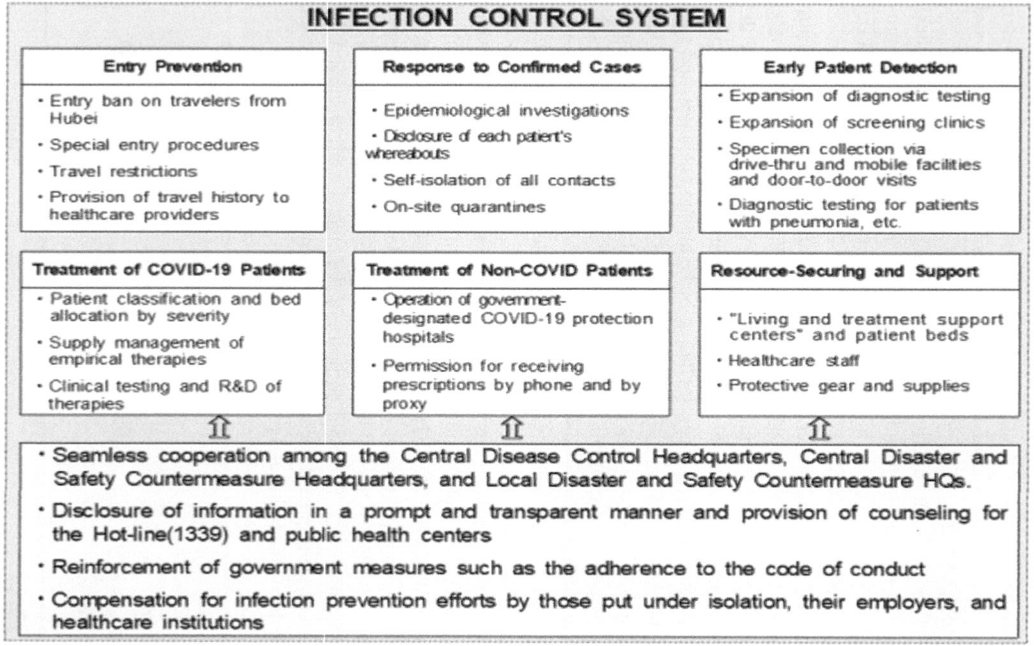

## INFECTION CONTROL SYSTEM

### Entry Prevention

- Entry ban on travelers from Hubei
- Special entry procedures
- Travel restrictions
- Provision of travel history to healthcare providers

### Response to Confirmed Cases

- Epidemiological investigations
- Disclosure of each patient's whereabouts
- Self-isolation of all contacts
- On-site quarantines

### Early Patient Detection

- Expansion of diagnostic testing
- Expansion of screening clinics
- Specimen collection via drive-thru and mobile facilities and door-to-door visits
- Diagnostic testing for patients with pneumonia, etc.

### Treatment of COVID-19 Patients

- Patient classification and bed allocation by severity
- Supply management of empirical therapies
- Clinical testing and R&D of therapies

### Treatment of Non-COVID Patients

- Operation of government-designated COVID-19 protection hospitals
- Permission for receiving prescriptions by phone and by proxy

### Resource-Securing and Support

- "Living and treatment support centers" and patient beds
- Healthcare staff
- Protective gear and supplies

- Seamless cooperation among the Central Disease Control Headquarters, Central Disaster and Safety Countermeasure Headquarters, and Local Disaster and Safety Countermeasure HQs.
- Disclosure of information in a prompt and transparent manner and provision of counseling for the Hot-line(1339) and public health centers
- Reinforcement of government measures such as the adherence to the code of conduct
- Compensation for infection prevention efforts by those put under isolation, their employers, and healthcare institutions

*Figure 5.4* Infection control system of Korea. *Source:* The Republic of Korea (March 31, 2020), "Tackling COVID-19: Health Quarantine and Economic Measures of South Korea".

The breakdown of the budget is as follows:

1. Health care system support: 5.2 trillion won was allocated for supporting the health care system, including funding for additional hospital beds, medical equipment and supplies, and compensation for medical staff.
2. Economic relief measures: 7.6 trillion won was allocated for economic relief measures, including direct cash payments to households, subsidies for small and medium-sized enterprises (SMEs), and support for job creation.
3. Quarantine and prevention measures: 1.5 trillion won was allocated for strengthening quarantine and prevention measures, including funding for COVID-19 testing and contact tracing, as well as support for the development of vaccines and treatments.

The central government was also active in forming policy networks in the form of committees. In October 2021, it created the Everyday Life Recovery Support Committee to gather opinions from various fields such as local governments, the business community, the cultural and sports sector, the education sector, and the medical sector to ease social distancing measures and prepare for the post-COVID era. The committee consists of 40 representatives and experts from the private and public sectors who are divided into four subcommittees, covering economy and public welfare, society and culture, administration and safety, and quarantine and health care. The Everyday Life Recovery Support Committee in Korea performed various roles in response to COVID-19. Its most significant role was to expand the communication channels between the government and citizens and provide feedback on policies. To achieve this, it held regular meetings and consulted with administrative officials to develop response measures. It also provided various policies and guidelines for the normalization of economic and social activities and developed an objective assessment of the normalization situation through the development of everyday life recovery indicators.

There are various actors within the central government, and not all of them necessarily agree with every policy decision. The Ministry of Health and Welfare constantly called for an increase in medical personnel, while the Ministry of Interior and Security provided active support by supplying medical personnel to public health centers. However, the latter faced opposition from the former when trying to reduce the number of medical personnel to the pre-pandemic level. There were also conflicts over role division between the Ministry of Health and Welfare and the KCDC after the latter was promoted to an independent agency. The Ministry of Education preferred to quickly resume offline classes, in contrast to the Ministry of Health and Welfare, which favored prolonging the aggressive quarantine measures. The Ministry of Science and ICT saw the crisis as an opportunity to promote digital transformation and suggested active digital transformation policies while requesting budget increases. The Ministry of Planning and Finance, responsible for the budget, expressed concerns about the rapidly increasing budget expenditures and maintained a tense relationship with other departments. Various perspectives held by different ministries within the government were shared and discussed during meetings of the State Council or the Central Disaster and Safety Countermeasure Headquarters. Since no ministry had a clear understanding of the future state during a disaster, it was not easy to present new policies actively rather than making conservative decisions to maintain the current situation, nor was it easy to convince other departments. Ultimately, issues that could not be resolved through inter-ministerial discussions were resolved through coordination by the Prime Minister's Office or the President's Office.

Each ministry of the central government in Korea primarily performs planning and policymaking functions, but there is a need for organizations that can execute these policies. In Korea, public institutions mainly execute their ministries' policies. The public institutions are defined in accordance with the Act on the Management of Public Institutions (Article 4) and refer to institutions established and operated by the government's investment, injection, or financial support that meet certain requirements designated annually by the Minister of Planning and Finance. As of 2022, there are 350 public institutions in Korea, employing approximately 440,000 people. These public institutions are subordinate organizations of the ministries and carry out activities to execute the policies of the ministries. During the COVID-19 response process, public institutions played a role in complying with and executing the government's quarantine policies, enabling prompt government responses. For example, the Korea Social Security Information Service, and the Small Enterprise and Market Service assessed the situation of households or small businesses affected by COVID-19 and provided government disaster relief funds. Of course, the government can consider contracting out to private companies to implement policies.

However, there are several potential advantages to using public institutions to implement public policies of the government, compared to contracting out to private companies. First of all, public institutions have a greater sense of public values and responsibility. As public institutions are established and operated by the government, they may have a greater sense of responsibility to the public. At the same time, they are more closely aligned with the government's policy goals than private companies, which are primarily focused on maximizing profits. Second, accountability and transparency can be well-secured. Internally, the sense of public values and responsibility makes public institutions more accountable and, externally, they are subject to oversight and accountability mechanisms of the government. As a result, public institutions can build up public trust and confidence in disaster response policies. Third, public institutions may have greater expertise in public policy areas: since public institutions are often established to address specific public policy areas, they may have greater expertise in those areas than private companies.

This expertise may enable them to better design and implement policies that achieve the government's goals.

To conclude, while the central government's COVID-19 response policies may appear to be planned, decided, and executed by a single organization, the response policies, in reality, can be considered as the result of interactions between various ministries and public institutions. This is because the COVID-19 response cannot be accomplished solely through health and medical policies. In this regard, the image of the central government that performs rational decision-making with a single purpose is quite different from reality. When understanding the central government as an actor in policy networks, one must fully consider these various aspects within the central government. Otherwise, there is a risk of falling into the trap of oversimplified logic.

### 5.1.3 Civil Society

Although the central government is the most prominent actor in the COVID-19 response network, we can find the collection of individuals, organizations, and institutions that operate outside of the government and the private sector called 'civil society', which tries to promote social, cultural, and political interests and values. Korea's civil society has undergone significant development through its democratization efforts. During the authoritarian rule of Park, Chung-hee from 1961 to 1979, civil society was suppressed, and non-governmental organizations (NGOs) were heavily controlled. However, as Korea democratized, civil society began to flourish, with NGOs becoming increasingly prominent. After democratization in the late 1980s, Korea's civil society has continued to grow and diversify. As of 2021, according to the Ministry of Interior and Safety, around 15,458 NGOs are officially registered in Korea and the number continuously grows. NGOs have become involved in a wide range of issues, including human rights, environmental protection, women's rights, labor rights, and education. Many NGOs have also worked to address the challenges faced by marginalized communities such as immigrants, disabilities, LGBTQ+, North Korean defectors, etc.

The role of civil society is not much highlighted compared to the activities of the government during the disaster response. However, in the aftermath of natural disasters such as earthquakes, floods, and typhoons, civil society organizations have been active in providing support and assistance to affected communities in Korea. One example of civil society involvement in disaster management in Korea is the work of volunteer organizations. These organizations, which include groups such as the Korean National Red Cross and the Korea Disaster Relief Association, provide emergency services and support to affected communities, such as distributing food and supplies, providing temporary shelter, and offering emotional support to survivors.

Civil society organizations in Korea also work closely with government agencies in disaster management. For example, NGOs have worked with the government to provide disaster relief and reconstruction efforts following major natural disasters, and have also collaborated with government agencies to develop disaster management policies and programs.

Around 160,000 volunteers joined the response activities, including disinfection and sterilization, public relations, consultation, supporting the quarantined, and distribution and production of masks, between January 20 and March 17, 2020. The volunteers worked with the Korean government for the intensive disinfection and sterilization of public spaces, which reduced the burden of civil servants and medical staff. They also provided food delivery, helped the elderly, made masks, and disseminated information useful for residents. Table 5.1 shows the number of volunteers by region and activities. As can be seen in Table 5.1, not only in densely populated areas such as Seoul and Gyeonggi province, but also throughout the country, many volunteers participated in various quarantine activities. This tradition of volunteerism did not suddenly emerge. In December 2007, the Hebei Spirit oil spill disaster, which involved the leakage of 10,547 cubic meters of oil from a tanker, occurred. At that time, nearly 1.23 million volunteers nationwide participated in the restoration work of the affected areas, contributing greatly to the popularization of volunteer activities. This tradition of volunteerism has also been introduced into the school education curriculum, and volunteering by elementary, middle, and high school students has become more common. While some still argue that the scale of volunteerism is not large, volunteer activities organized during crises have greatly contributed to raising public awareness of COVID-19 prevention efforts.

The other important group was the association of medical doctors and nurses. According to the Korean Nurses Association, around 4,000 nurses (almost 2% of Korea's practicing nurses) volunteered in Daegu in March 2020. Medical doctors shared information about the situation of COVID-19 through social network services. Their exchange of ideas resulted in the adoption of a drive-through test and residential treatment center.

The volunteering activities have continued since March 2020. More than 660,000 volunteered by June 23, 2020, and participated in a variety of response activities such as making face masks, communicable disease control, and helping those in need (The Prime Minister's Office Press Release on July 10, 2020). The volunteer's activities were strategically organized through the volunteer organizations' network in which nonprofit organizations worked closely with the Ministry of Interior and Safety.

The technological innovation was initiated by civilian experts who voluntarily organized a team for developing so-called mask apps. Facing the skyrocketing demand for facial masks, the Korean government announced that it would control the distribution of masks. The policy was implemented on March 5, 2020, and this was so that each person could only purchase two masks per week, but it proved to be difficult to establish a computerized system that could identify who bought how many masks from which pharmacy.

Table 5.1 The number of volunteers (between January 20 and March 17)

| Region | Total (person) | Activity type (person) | | | | | | |
|---|---|---|---|---|---|---|---|---|
| | | Disinfection and sterilization | Public relations | Consultation | Supporting the quarantined | Distribution of masks | Production of masks | ETC |
| Seoul (March 10) | 19,065 | 10,224 | 5,657 | 1,407 | 9 | 347 | 908 | 513 |
| Busan | 18,307 | 10,288 | 937 | 252 | 155 | 1,261 | 5,059 | 355 |
| Daegu | 1,209 | 317 | 78 | 204 | 8 | 359 | 138 | 105 |
| Incheon (March 10) | 1,136 | 597 | – | – | – | – | 482 | 57 |
| Gwangju | 15,111 | 12,337 | 1,159 | – | 46 | – | 1,236 | 333 |
| Daejeon (March 10) | 263 | 21 | – | – | – | – | 183 | 59 |
| Ulsan | 5,180 | 2,915 | 389 | 98 | 0 | 103 | 734 | 941 |
| Sejong | 558 | 217 | 68 | – | 8 | 36 | – | 229 |
| Gyunggi | 33,521 | 18,275 | 3,670 | 150 | 75 | 3,317 | 5,778 | 2,256 |
| Kangwon | 8,960 | 3,088 | 422 | 84 | 7 | 428 | 4,135 | 796 |
| Chungbuk | 6,549 | 3,835 | 178 | 3 | – | 228 | 1,432 | 873 |
| Chungnam | 5,450 | 1,753 | 567 | 25 | 7 | 283 | 2,212 | 603 |
| Jeonbuk | 5,605 | 2,142 | 515 | – | 28 | 806 | 1,222 | 892 |
| Jeonnam | 8,104 | 3,777 | 1,099 | 326 | – | 211 | 2,346 | 345 |
| Gyeongbuk | 17,238 | 13,644 | 1,542 | 22 | 250 | 217 | 1,377 | 186 |
| Gyeongnam | 6,131 | 750 | 439 | – | – | 296 | 3,005 | 1,641 |
| Jeju | 9,416 | 6,653 | 919 | 82 | 2 | 715 | 944 | 101 |
| Total | 161,803 | 90,833 | 17,639 | 2,653 | 595 | 8,607 | 31,191 | 10,285 |

*Source*: Ministry of Interior and Safety, Press release, March 27, 2020.

Moreover, it was not possible to know how many masks were left in each pharmacy, which caused enormous confusion. It was judged that it would take more than three months for the government to develop an app that identified mask sales and pharmacy stocks. However, private software experts argued that if the government provided information on pharmacy location and sales volume, it would be possible to develop a mask app that citizens could easily use. Embracing the experts' suggestion, the government was able to quickly supply mask apps to citizens through collaboration with these private experts. What is worth noting is that a private company provides a server that can handle the mask app service that tens of millions of people access every day, and the initially developed mask app goes through a competitive process for a certain period of time before being integrated around the mask app provided by platform operators.

Despite the importance of civil society, it also has some limitations. The advantage of civic organizations is that they allow diverse individuals having different resources and experts to participate in disaster management. However, it is not easy to coordinate the activities of various civic organizations having different purposes, scales, expertise, and participation methods. Some civic organizations often oppose the government's disaster policies, and there are many conflicts among civic organizations with different political orientations or conflicting interests. In some cases, small civic organizations may lack continuity and responsibility. An organized civil society can check the power and resources concentrated in the government during a disaster situation, and protect the freedom and rights of citizens from the government's infringement. The role of civic organizations in disaster response should not be limited to supplementing the government's inadequate service capacity. Civil society creates a social atmosphere that can overcome disasters by sharing crisis awareness in the early stages of a disaster, raising awareness of social solidarity among citizens, and providing political support or checks necessary for disaster responses. Considering these limitations and possibilities, the government needs to respect the autonomy of civil society and cooperate with civic organizations as important partners in policy networks. In fact, various academic societies or associations composed of health care professionals have actively explored and shared COVID-related response measures with the government, and local civic organizations have also formed networks for mutual cooperation. Especially in the initial stages, various small to medium-sized groups attempted independent activities but quickly formed various network structures within civil society. Therefore, the criticism that the existence of diverse citizen organizations will lead to disorderly disaster response is not valid.

### 5.1.4 Local Government

Local governments played as the first respondents and detected the seriousness of disease spread much earlier than the central government. When the second wave of COVID-19 spread on February 18, 2020, in Daegu, the Mayor of Daegu, Kwon, Youngjin, quickly realized the seriousness of the community's infection. He convened meetings with the local health center, board of education, police, and military to find ways to deal with the rising infection. On February 20, he requested the central government to raise the alert level from Orange to Red and the central government accepted the request on February 23.

The epicenter of the disease was the city of Daegu and North Gyeongsang province, which accounted for almost 77% of the total confirmed cases throughout the country (as of April, 30).[5] On March 15, the government declared special disaster areas status for Daegu city and Gyeongsan city/Cheongdo county/Bonghwa County, located within Gyeongsang province. According to the Framework Act on the Management of Disaster and Safety Article 61, once an area is declared as a special disaster area, the central or local governments may provide administrative, fiscal, financial, and medical support for the response, relief, and restoration activities.

Though not as much exposed to the disease compared to Daegu and Gyeongbuk, the spread of the virus in Seoul, the capital city of Korea, and Gyeonggi was of great concern since almost 50% of the total population is densely populated around these areas. In the business sector, major private companies have made decisions to have some of their employees work from home since February although it was not enforced. Various measures were taken at the local level to prevent and slow down the spread of the disease. In Seoul, for instance, hand sanitizers and masks were provided without cost in public transportation; daily reports were made public through YouTube and the website; quarantine facilities were provided for those who needed special care, etc. Most of all, public health centers in Seoul reduced their normal functions and operated as COVID-19 screening centers, which contributed to expanding the number of people being tested.[6] As seen from the Seoul case, the local governments conducted preliminary investigations of the cases and then the central immediate response teams of the KCDC were dispatched to the regions experiencing immense outbreaks to proceed with the epidemiological investigations jointly with the local governments. These measures speeded up the accomplishment of investigations which would otherwise have delayed the process, resulting in ineffectiveness in February and April 2020.

One of the most critical roles of the local governments in the prevention of disease is to track and trace suspected patients and their contacts at the earlier stages.[7] One method utilized by the local governments was establishing a system that sends notifications to the residents, namely the Cellular Broadcasting Service (CBS). The fast-track processes were made possible since they didn't require the local governments to receive approval from the central government's Ministry of Interior and Safety (MOIS).[8] Along with that, a self-diagnosis mobile application was used as a channel through which the government could monitor inbound travelers. Since April 1, 2020, all of the inbound travelers had been asked to install mobile applications: a self-diagnosis application and a self-quarantine safety application (a self-quarantine safety application includes the functions of self-diagnosis). The data submitted by the users on their symptoms are then shared with the local governments and public health centers.

The lessons learned from MERS in 2015 were that the development of community-wide surveillance system, public–private collaboration, and networks among agencies to transfer the patients were significant factors to maintain the capacity for a community in prevention and response.[9] Of all, the prevention of the disease is largely impacted by how well the surveillance system is established so as not to have delays due to lack of information. When an individual tests positive for COVID-19, the medical institution that conducted the test is required to report the case to the local government of the patient's place of residence. The local government then conducts an epidemiological investigation to identify the patient's close contacts and potential transmission routes. When close contacts are identified, they are put on self-quarantine, during which periods the quarantined persons are monitored by assigned staff of the Ministry of Interior and Safety.[10] Local governments share information about the confirmed and quarantined patients with the KCDC and the public health centers within the jurisdictions.

When COVID-19 broke out in January 2020, if an infection case was detected, the local government reported the case to the KCDC and waited until the KCDC sent a quarantine inspector. Such a practice was based on the assumption that the local government is not capable of systematic investigation. However, the practice did not work as there were too many cases to investigate quickly. So, on February 27, 2020, the Korean government changed the procedure to 'investigation first, report later'. According to the revised rule, the local governments could do a preliminary investigation and quarantine and report the case to the KCDC later.

The reporting system, which yielded the first response authority to the local, could partly be attributed to learning from the past. In the tragic ferry Sewol disaster in 2014, the government was harshly criticized for its ineffective response which resulted in the loss of hundreds of lives. One of the factors that delayed actual response activities at the field was the multilayered reporting procedures that could have been used to save lives. Since then, the Korean government implemented various measures, including organizational reform. By applying 'investigation first, report later', local governments were able to rapidly respond without waiting until the central government gave appropriate orders.

The local governments also collaborated with each other. For instance, the city of Daegu had only 48 negative pressure isolation rooms on February 20, 2020, and it could not handle thousands of patients who needed special care. Some criticized the city government for not having more public hospitals, but this argument is seriously flawed given the fact that the supply exceeded the demand in the ordinary situation, which would cause additional deficits for the National Health Insurance. The solution that Daegu found was resource sharing with other local governments. For instance, Daegu sent 1,216 patients to almost 57 hospitals nationwide on April 7. Of course, the sharing of resources was possible because there were many provinces having negligible numbers of patients, and many citizens support their local government's decision to admit Daegu patients to their region's hospitals.

Local governments in Korea provided disaster relief funds tailored to their respective situations, separate from the disaster support funds provided by the central government. The size of this disaster relief fund varied greatly depending on the financial situation of each local government, and the method of selecting beneficiaries also differed. Gyeonggi Province, for instance, preferred to provide universal disaster relief funds to all residents, and the amount provided was much larger than that of other local governments. Some local governments provided the funds in the form of a 'local love gift voucher', while others used credit cards or bank deposits. The local love gift voucher is a type of voucher or coupon to support local businesses and boost the local economy. The voucher can be used to purchase goods and services from participating local businesses, such as restaurants, shops, and service providers. The goal is to encourage people to spend their money locally and support small businesses, which can help to create jobs and stimulate economic growth in the region. The voucher typically has an expiration date and may have certain restrictions on its use, such as a limit on the amount that can be spent per transaction.

Local governments also adopted different eligibility criteria for the relief fund but it was mainly determined based on household income, with the lower 80% of households based on health insurance premiums used as a standard. The difference in the size of support between local governments raised concerns for the central government about increasing regional disparities and the possibility of disaster relief funds being misused as a means for local government elections. In reality, the economic shock from COVID-19 in Korea was relatively small, and in 2022, the situation quickly recovered, but various local governments still increased the size of their disaster relief funds due to local elections and using COVID-19 as an excuse.

## 5.2 Transparency and Risk Communication through Information Sharing

Risk communication is critical to the efficient response to the disaster (Comfort, 2019; Moynihan, 2009) as the disaster response network consists of many actors, relations, and continuous interactions in which different resources and information are produced, exchanged, and used. Proper risk communication enhances the transparency of the government response policy but it is not as easy as we expect.

Infectious diseases are disasters with high uncertainty, so it is difficult for citizens to obtain accurate information. Claims that only information on the number of confirmed cases is underreporting the number of confirmed cases has been raised in countries around the world. Tanzania prevented the president from announcing the statistics of confirmed cases in May 2020 and even claimed that if you pray to God, you can overcome the COVID-19 virus. The fatality rate of COVID-19 also varied substantially according to country, and the government did not make an accurate announcement about the number of asymptomatic COVID-19 patients, making it difficult to judge the risk of COVID-19. Moreover, the controversy over the safety of vaccines was also a factor that increased the anxiety level of citizens. In such circumstances, it has become ever more important for the government to provide transparent information about the spread and risk of COVID-19.

One of the biggest misunderstandings about infectious disease-related statistics is to think that the measurement of confirmed cases or deaths can be done objectively. Even if only looking at the criteria for determining confirmed cases, there is a big difference in the sensitivity level, that is, the probability of determining an infected person as positive in the test, depending on the test method. Rapid antigen test (RAT) is less accurate in detecting actual positive patients. From December 2020 to April 2022, 5,496 emergency room patients who had both RAT and PCR tests were analyzed. As a result, of the 418 PCR test positives, only 239 were positive in the RAT test. In other words, the sensitivity, which is the probability of a positive test result among actually infected patients, was only about 57% in the case of RAT. Thus, the remaining 43% were negative on the RAT test, but turned out to be positive. Therefore, if the number of confirmed cases is determined using positive RAT test patients, the problem of underestimating the number of confirmed cases could potentially occur. On the other hand, there were only three cases in which the PCR test result was true and the RAT test. Therefore, if the RAT is positive, it is highly likely that the patient was actually positive.

It can also be argued that the positive detection rate may vary depending on the difference in cycle threshold (CT) value even if PCR testing is performed. It was argued that the number of confirmed cases in 2020 was low because the CT value was set to low in Korea. However, the appropriate CT value is set according to the situation of the diagnostic kit and is not set to artificially reduce the number of confirmed cases. Death statistics are also problematic. If a COVID-19 patient dies from a traffic accident or dies from complications after being cured of COVID-19, or if the main cause of death is another disease that had already existed, not a respiratory disease, although infected with COVID-19, the question is whether to determine it as a COVID-19 death.

Since Korea has adopted the National Health Insurance system, it was possible to obtain statistics of confirmed cases and deaths by presenting the same standards to all medical institutions. In the early days, there was a lot of confusion because these standards were unclear, but efforts were made to improve the accuracy of infectious disease statistics by continuously updating the guidelines. Experts also presented their opinions on the government's guidelines through lively discussions. Their acceptance of the government's guidelines was high. Regular disclosure of information contributed greatly to securing trust in the Korean government in the early stages. The KCDC commissioner provided statistics on confirmed cases and deaths and explained the government's quarantine policy at a regular briefing every day at 2:00 p.m.

The Korean data is made up of comprehensive tests. From the MERS experience, Korea learned the importance of detecting infected people as promptly as possible. Korea performed intensive tests despite the concern of costs and reporting more cases, which might weaken the political support of the government. As of April 27, 2020, almost 600,000 tests were done and few Koreans believe that the government hesitates to provide test services to hide information. Even though the event number of infection cases was small in April 2020, the Korean government encouraged comprehensive tests for any suspicious persons. Due to the comprehensive test policy, entire buildings or office users were recommended to take the COVID-19 test even if a single confirmed case was detected. This suggests that there was very little concern that the Korean government underreported the infection cases.

In addition, Korea adopts a consistent rule to confirm an infection. Some countries change their rules for confirming the infection over time but Korea uses the real-time PCR method that WHO adopts. The guideline for test, confirmation, and report was continuously revised responding to inquiries from hospitals and field agents of public organizations. Based on the guideline, local governments and hospitals report confirmed cases to the KCDC, and the information is released as of 0 a.m. In the early stage of COVID-19, the Korean government released data as of 9 a.m. and 4 p.m. each day. Reporting data twice would be good for getting the most recent information, but it also caused confusion among the people. Hence, the Korean government has announced the official statistics of 0 a.m. since March 2, 2020. At the same time, it holds a press conference at 10 a.m. to report the situation and response of the government.

The sharing of information is conducted through multiple channels. The primary formal channel for risk communication is the government's official response governance defined by the Infectious Disease Control and Prevention Act (IDCPA). According to the law, Korea's National Infectious Disease Risk Alert System has four levels, as shown in Figure 5.5. The response governance changes according to the risk alert level issued and adjusted by the Minister of Health and Welfare. At level 4, the Central Disaster and Safety Countermeasure Headquarter becomes the command center. The meeting chaired by the prime minister comprises all relevant ministries of the central government and heads of local governments. Between late February and late April 2020, meetings were held every day of the week with few exceptions

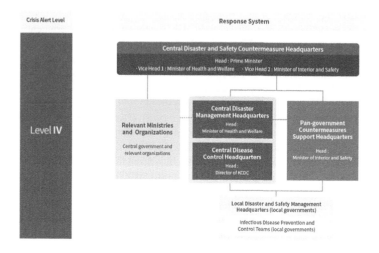

*Figure 5.5* The governance structure at risk alert level 4. *Source:* MOHW (2020).

MOHW (2020). The prime minister received a direct report from the local government heads and relevant ministries regarding the situation. As the prime minister gave the director an order to resolve problems, agile policy responses from the identification of problems and policy decisions to implementation were possible. Moreover, the meeting can open many communication channels among the leaders of governments, ministries, and agencies. Many local government heads argue that the prime minister's meetings helped resolve the shortage of equipment and contact tracing experts.

The major channels of risk communication are CBS, press releases, and government briefings. Table 5.2 indicates key information delivered via major channels of information (Lee et al., 2020). The data is based on 9,100 CBS, 156 government briefings, and 438 press releases from January 20 to May 5 (Lee et al., 2020). Information associated with confirmed cases ranked highest in all three channels. Other types of information conveyed were information on government support policies, response operations, and prevention of the disease.

The CBS, in particular, serves as an initial alarm that notifies the public about the risk they are facing and guidelines for further actions. As the CBS is delivered to all mobile phone users far more comprehensively than the normal SMS text messaging system, it avoids the possibility of being uninformed. From January 20 to May 5, 2020, the number of emergency text messages sent by the central and local government through CBS regarding COVID-19 was 9,100, and 43.1% provided information on the infected cases (Lee et al., 2020).

*Table 5.2* Key information delivered in major channels of communication

| Rank | Cellular broadcasting system | | Press release | | Government briefing | |
|---|---|---|---|---|---|---|
| 1 | Information related to the confirmed cases | 43.1% | Information related to the confirmed cases | 30.7% | Information related to the confirmed cases | 40.0% |
| 2 | Information on response to the disease | 34.5% | Information on government support policies | 24.5% | Information on government support policies | 36.8% |
| 3 | Information on the prevention of the spread | 17.6% | Information on response to the disease | 13.6% | Information on the prevention of the spread | 19.6% |
| 4 | Information on government support policies | 4.8% | Information on prevention of the spread | 11.7% | Information on response of the disease | 3.6% |

*Source:* Lee et al. (2020).

The Ministry of Health and Welfare (MOHW) made use of digital media and provided live daily briefings through YouTube and Facebook. The Ministry of Trade, Industry, and Energy communicated with the public through SNS to correct misinformation about COVID-19.

The other channels of risk communication are the media and some experts' COVID-19 apps and websites. The information provided by the government to the press was not immediately available for statistical analysis but was in the form of a PDF or document file, which meant that it was difficult to analyze the long-term trend of the spread. Also, in terms of speed, it took time to collect the information announced by each region. In order to solve this problem, some private experts collected the statistics of COVID-19 confirmed cases and deaths announced by each local government in real time and released the COVID-19 situation to the public faster than the official statistics of KCDC and in turn received a great response. The COVID-19 app developed by the private sector had a problem due to insufficient server capacity as the number of users exploded, but this problem was solved with voluntary donations from citizens, and statistical errors were quickly corrected using information shared by users.

The Asia Regional Information Center at Seoul National University developed a website aimed at providing diverse information essential for determining policies related to COVID-19. The information presented includes the number of available hospital beds, the number of severely ill patients, the vaccination rate, the use of public transportation, and the utilization of cultural facilities. Additionally, the website presents statistics on confirmed cases and deaths, all of which are accessible to the public. Such private efforts have significantly aided in preventing the spread of misinformation related to COVID-19 and facilitated a more measured response from the public.

The rapidity with which the private sector was able to provide COVID-19-related information can be attributed to the use of an e-government platform built by Korean public institutions, which has enabled quick collection, integration, and processing of data utilizing open API technology and various data crawling techniques. The increase in public access to established databases has enabled the private sector to exercise their creativity and develop services for citizens that the government was unable to provide. Consequently, the sharing of COVID-19-related information has increased, leading to enhanced policy transparency. This approach to data management is akin to building a system for disaster management, constructing an ecological system that creates and shares information necessary for responding to disasters by connecting naturally produced data resulting from administrative tasks.

Private sector involvement has been critical in providing this information promptly. The e-government platform built by Korean public institutions has enabled rapid data collection, integration, and processing. Increased access to established databases has facilitated private sector creativity in developing citizen services that enhance policy transparency. The approach adopted can be likened to constructing a disaster management system, creating an ecological system that connects naturally produced data resulting from administrative tasks for disaster response purposes.

Another point to note regarding the transparency of the policy is the 'Everyday Life Recovery Support Committee' activity that started from October 2021. The committee, co-chaired by the prime minister and private experts, and composed of 8 government and 30 private members, reviewed policies to ease social distancing as vaccinations were actively conducted and the spread of COVID-19 decreased. This committee played a role in collecting opinions from various social classes, such as small business owners, universities, and the culture sector, who were suffering from COVID-19, as well as infectious disease experts and local governments. In this committee, the government decided on a policy direction by gathering various opinions rather than making a policy decision unilaterally and then sharing it with the committee participants. Through face-to-face meetings once every two weeks, discussions were held in the direction of easing the social distancing policy while sharing opinions with each other. As a result, in November the committee announced that the social distancing policy was eased. The decision was revoked in December 2021 because the Omicron mutation spread again. The reason why the country returned to the previous social distancing policy within a short period of time was that some experts who were hesitant to ease the social distancing policy heavily criticized the government's easing policy by emphasizing the skyrocketing infection cases due to the Omicron variant. In contrast, groups advocating for the relaxation of the social distancing policy raised objections that it was not necessary to continue the social distancing policy simply because there were more infection cases, as long as sufficient hospital beds were secured and the severity rate and fatality rate were not high. Opinions regarding whether to ease social distancing measures differed among medical experts, economic and administrative experts, and even within government departments. This indicates that there were groups that would not agree with any decision made. Information shared with experts by the Everyday Life Recovery Support Committee such as the number of severe patients, fatality rate, and available hospital beds, as well as opinions from small business owners and frontline education institutions, helped understand each other's decisions.

The fear of the COVID-19 vaccine can be lowered by sharing transparent information. According to the KCDC, since the first COVID-19 vaccine was administered on February 26, 2021, a total of 482,451 adverse events have been reported over a period of 100 weeks. Of these, 96.0% (462,990 cases) were categorized as common adverse events, 3.6% (17,518 cases) as serious adverse events, and 0.4% (1,943 cases) as fatal. Despite a significant number of reported adverse events, Korea was able to achieve a vaccination rate of over 95% due to the transparent reporting of information regarding COVID-19 vaccine adverse events every two weeks. This practice of transparent reporting of adverse events is significant in promoting trust and confidence in vaccination programs. Without proper reporting of COVID-19 vaccine side effects, individuals may be hesitant to get vaccinated, potentially leading to low vaccination rates and increased risk of disease transmission. By contrast, providing timely and accurate information about the potential risks and benefits of vaccines can help individuals make informed decisions about their health and encourage them to participate in vaccination programs. In this way, transparent reporting of COVID-19 vaccine side effects plays an important role in maintaining public health and preventing the spread of infectious diseases.

At the same time, the KCDC established the "Korean Vaccine Injury Compensation Program" to provide compensation to individuals who suffer from the severe side effects of COVID-19 vaccines. This compensation program, which was implemented in July 2021, has incentivized the reporting of adverse events related to COVID-19 vaccines, as it provides financial support for individuals who experience severe reactions. Hence, the government can prevent the underreporting of adverse effect cases. The significance of gathering COVID-19 vaccine side effect statistics is that it allows for the identification of potential safety concerns related to the vaccines. By closely monitoring the reported adverse events, health authorities can quickly investigate and respond to any safety concerns, and take appropriate actions to ensure the safety and efficacy of the vaccines.

In addition, publicly available data on COVID-19 vaccine side effects can help to build trust and confidence in the vaccine, as it provides transparency and accountability in the vaccination process. This can ultimately help to increase vaccine uptake and contribute to the overall control of the COVID-19 pandemic.

Overall, the Korean government appears to have been successful in maintaining the transparency of information as a result of experiencing MERS. Organizational efforts – from creating the Office of Communication within the KCDC to institutionalizing SOPs on risk communication – indicate how much the government was willing to communicate with the public after they had recognized the risk. Furthermore, during COVID-19, the government was flexible enough to involve other actors to develop methods of information-sharing. Such a coordinated, multi-actor effort to create valid and useful information stimulated the development of information-sharing platforms with the help of ICT. The observations of the first six months of COVID-19 teach us that the role of the government in risk communication is to create and filter information. As the information provided by the government accumulated, the citizens and private sectors voluntarily developed websites and services including visualization of the Corona Map, a real-time update board of infected cases, networks of transmissions overtime, etc.

## 5.3　Information Communication Technologies

The ICT played a significant role in providing general information on the progress of pandemic, tracing the contracts, distributing face masks, and monitoring international travelers. Besides, the ICT helped the government collect information, support decisions, and improve the quality of response policies. Some examples using ICTs are, for example, telemedicine, contact-tracing apps, virtual meeting and conference tools, health-monitoring wearables, robotics and drones, and numerous websites reporting the status of infections.

Korea is well known for its very stringent privacy policy. The Personal Information Protection Act (PIPA) of 2011 requires the consent of individuals before collecting, using, and disclosing personal information. Korea, however, had a negative experience with MERS in 2015 and enacted the Contagious Disease Prevention and Control Act (CDPCA), which allows the government to use private information to collect seven types of data: location; immigration records; closed-circuit television footage; credit, debit, and prepaid card transaction; transit-pass record; personal identification record; and prescription and medical records (Park et al., 2020). Figure 5.6 shows the structure of data collection and distribution within the Korean government.

The contact tracing system for identifying individuals who have had close contact with confirmed COVID-19 cases in Korea is composed of various data sources. Location information was obtained from mobile phones, while information on arrivals was confirmed through immigration records.

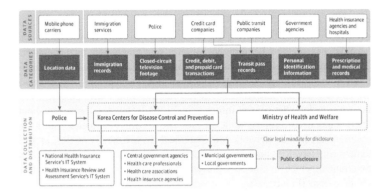

*Figure 5.6* COVID-19 contact tracking system in Korea. *Source:* Park et al. (2020).

The police provided CCTV information, credit card companies provided transaction data, and public transportation companies provided information on card usage for tracking movement. The government confirmed personal information, while the KCDC and the Health and Welfare Ministry provided databases of medical prescriptions and health care information. This information was integrated through the databases of the police, the KCDC, and the Ministry of Health and Welfare, and was then shared with the central and local governments and medical facilities for use in managing close contacts. This process allowed for the quick identification of close contacts through information and communication technology. However, due to the extensive sharing of personal information, this process raised concerns regarding conflicts with Korea's Personal Information Protection Act. The IDCPA enabled such information-sharing during the spread of infectious diseases.

The utilization of ICT significantly reduced the time for tracking the contacts of COVID-19 patients. In the early stage of COVID-19, the KCDC had to trace contacts of the infected people manually. However, the government shortened the time to 10 minutes after developing the COVID-19 Smart Management System (SMS) which analyzes data from 28 public as well as private organizations such as credit card companies, smartphone companies, etc. As the contact information is also sent to people through cell phones, it prevents secondary infection. As a result, citizens who were at the same places with the infected could quarantine themselves and go to the hospital for a test, not incurring further infections.

Information is shared via mobile phones, internet as well as traditional media such as newspapers or TV. Korea has past experiences of natural disasters such as the Gyeongju earthquake (on September 12, 2016) and Gangneung Forest fire (on May 6, 2017). In coping with the disasters, the

Korean government realized that while warning and urgent information was sent to the public via short text messages and mass media by the government, it took a long time to do so due to many steps of bureaucratic approvals and technical problems. During the disasters, the Korean government improved the efficiency of the CBS through which it sent emergency alert messages simultaneously to millions of mobile users. In terms of the Gyeongju earthquake, it took 6 minutes to send the message, but one year later, the time was reduced to around 7–25 seconds in 2018, which is a significant progress. The messages include the contact information of the infected, information about newly announced response policies, etc. The MOIS collaborates with local governments, mobile network providers, and most Koreans as well as foreigners who have cell phones and can receive the official messages from the government, which significantly prevents the possibility of the spread of fear and fake news (Figure 5.7).

The innovative responses based on technologies come from the private sector. As the number of new cases had increased in mid-February, many hospitals were concerned that their medical resources were running out. If a patient turned out to be infected by COVID-19, all medical staff who contacted the patients were to be quarantined, and the building was to be closed to prevent secondary infections. Hence, some private hospitals hesitated to take people who wanted to take a test. Moreover, it took a couple of hours from the entry to finish the test due to extra caution to prevent possible infection of people in the building. The drive-thru system which significantly reduces the time to 10 minutes was invented by the experts and a local government, not by the central government.

The distribution of masks was also successfully conducted by utilizing IT. The short supply of masks and uprising prices became a social problem in

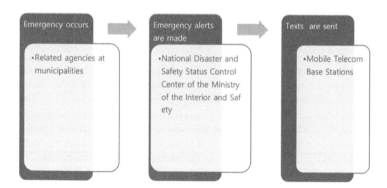

*Figure 5.7* The sequences of sending emergency messages. *Source:* The Republic of Korea (2020), "How Korea responded to a pandemic using ICT flattening the curve on COVID-19," p.8.

mid-February. The government decided to ask the mask companies to provide up to 80% of their mask production and it distributed them to the public. As the mask should be given to all equally, the government utilized the residential ID and the Health Insurance Review and Assessment Service in order to prevent individuals from purchasing too many masks. At the same time, the data became linked with pharmacies and post offices to share the inventory and sales data. Moreover, people had to wait in long lines when the public mask provision was done on February 28, 2020, the line was quickly shortened after providing the apps locating the pharmacies and their inventory.

Various forms of technologies were also used for the 'intact' service such as telemedicine (remote Medicare), thermal image cameras, internet delivery systems, and online education. Due to the nature of contagious disease, the best preventive method to reduce the infection is to reduce the contact, and technologies make life without contact feasible. The SK group allowed their employees to work from home on February 25 and Hyundai, Hanwha, and other major companies also adopted it later. On March 12, the Ministry of Personnel Management (MPS) released the "Guidelines for Flexible Work Hours among Civil Servants to Tackle COVID-19", which 55 ministries and agencies of the central government mandated their employees work from home through the use of a Global Virtual Private Network (GVPN).[11] As the guideline requested more than one-third of the total number of employees in each department to work remotely on a rotating basis, all public servants had the experience of working from home.

Remote Medicare began to be utilized. Korea is famous for adopting new information technologies but telemedicine was not allowed due to the heavy resistance by doctors, whose concern was the decrease in medical service quality and the profit of hospitals. Some innovative start-ups already developed advanced technologies but could not use them on the market due to regulation. However, COVID-19 changed the regulation policy. When Daegu City had an increasing number of infection cases, many citizens started to call the 1339 hotline to have a COVID-19 test as they could not visit hospitals without the diagnosis of a doctor on the 1339 hotline. Unfortunately, the hotline was so busy that the government had to conceive new approaches. Moreover, non-COVID-19 patients who had to visit hospitals could not do so as many hospitals had to take care of serious COVID-19 patients. To alleviate the bottleneck, the Korean government temporarily approved telemedicine on February 24. As a result, more than 104,000 prescriptions were issued by telemedicine by April 12. Also, the Coronavirus 119 app and other applications were developed and to make citizens access the remote medical services.

The adoption of ICTs for responding to COVID-19 was able to be implemented from former lessons learnt, namely, the MERS in 2015 which affected 186 people and caused 36 deaths in Korea (OECD/KDI, 2018; Kim et al., 2017). The failure of communication during MERS led to amendments to the IDCPA for timely detection, decision-making, and information-sharing among authorities and citizens (OECD, 2020). Those changes enabled the Korean government to use Global Positioning System (GPS) location data from mobile phone records, credit card transactions, and CCTV footage for tracing the patients' contacts in conducting epidemiological investigations for COVID-19 (Park et al., 2020), shutting down and disinfecting places located on the patients' movement paths.

Based on the IDCPA amended after MERS, the Korean government was able to actively use ICTs. First, the Korean government sent emergency text alerts about spikes of infections in their local area. Using tracking information and data provided by national, provincial, and local governments, nongovernmental actors voluntarily developed user-friendly apps and websites that did not require people to have data literacy skills to identify the risks of COVID-19 in their lives. For example, a college student developed the website Corona Map (http://coronamap.site/), which allowed people to see the location of new infections and up-to-date data on COVID-19 based on their location. The rapid popularity of Corona Map caused the server to crash, and as a result private online platform companies – Naver, Kakao Corporation, and Amazon Web Service (AWS) – funded the website (Lee et al., 2021). Combining the geolocation information of smartphone and internet users with the data provided by KCDC and local governments, the apps and websites disseminated necessary information on COVID-19 to the public and encouraged people to make behavioral changes to reduce their exposure to risks.

However, proactive strategies of contact tracing and surveillance amplified privacy concerns. In the earlier phase of the outbreak, personal information such as gender, nationality, and age of the infected were made public through the MOHFW website. Even though personal information collected pursuant to Article 76-2 of the IDCPA was protected from disclosure by the PIPA, some of the local governments and municipalities disclosed more detailed information such that individuals were identifiable when the individual pieces of information were aggregated. Recognizing the seriousness of the issue, Korea's National Human Rights Commission suggested that the information on the contacts of the infected should be limited to the places they had visited rather than revealing individuals' identifiable information (March 9, 2020).

One of the difficulties in maintaining consistency with regard to protecting privacy while tracking the contacts was that the local governments had different standards for disclosing individuals' information. For example, the city of Bucheon did not reveal the name of the store that the infected person visited, whereas Seoul did. Thus, to improve the consistency and protect the disclosure of personal information, on March 14, 2020, KCDC distributed 'The guideline for disclosure of information on tracing the path of the infected' to local governments and municipalities. These guidelines strictly prohibited disclosure of identifiable personal information. Accordingly, most local governments stopped disclosing workplace addresses and home addresses.

Despite the guidelines, some local governments still violated the guidelines for collecting, publicizing, and keeping personal information. KCDC made further two revisions to the guidelines, on April 12 and June 30, 2020; these revisions explained when governments could release personal information to the public and what information they could disclose or not disclose. Published on June 30, 2020, the third set of guidelines specified that governments must not release personally identifiable information, aiming to balance control of the spread of the virus with privacy concerns.

In the airport, travelers had to take a COVID-19 test and were sent to special quarantine facilities if the test result came out positive. Short-term travelers with negative test results were also asked to be quarantined in the special quarantine facilities. All international travelers were to install the COVID-19 Self-Quarantine Safety Protection App on their cell phones and report their health condition throughout the 14 days. The app used GPS and tracked the locations of those in self-quarantine to ensure that they did not leave their quarantine areas without permission. Even if travelers were exempted from quarantine with a diplomatic or an official government visa, or a Quarantine Exemption Certificate issued by the Korean Embassy or Consulate-General prior to the entry, they had to install the Self-Diagnosis App to be monitored by the MOHW (MOHW, 2020a) (Figure 5.8).

The Korean government paid for the test costs and delivered the necessities and food to those who were being quarantined. According to the Ministry of Interior and Safety, among the 324,600 quarantined people, the reported violation cases of control rules were only 0.16% between February 19 and June 10, 2020.[12] Such high compliance is very impressive given that Korea employed a far more voluntary approach compared to China or other European countries that adopted a lockdown policy.

As the spread of COVID-19 progressed, ICT technology was actively used to identify and support economically struggling households. As it was difficult to identify households in need through individual visits, the Korea Social Security Information Service (SSIS) identified power cuts, water supply cuts, excessive expenditure on medical expenses, arrears on health insurance fees, arrears on public housing rent, a system to identify vulnerable households using information such as income and property was established in 2018. In the

*Figure 5.8* QR codes for self-quarantine safety protection app. *Source:* For Entrants to Korea: Instructions for Quarantine Subjects, provided by KCDC and distributed by the Ministry of Foreign Affairs. (https://overseas.mofa.go.kr/).

process of building this system, a system and technical foundation that was able to link information from various institutions was established, and this information linkage was able to be done quickly in the process of responding to COVID-19. As a result, SSIS established the 'COVID-19 Response Hub System' to integrate COVID-19-confirmed patient information generated by KCDC, HIRA, National Health Insurance Service (NHIS), Korea Health Information Service, etc., to notify confirmed cases and quarantine procedure notification. This made it possible to significantly reduce the cost of managing confirmed patients by rapidly integrating confirmed patient information collected at the individual hospital, local government, and public health center level. Additionally, it was possible to promptly provide disaster relief funds by using the information on vulnerable groups collected by SSIS.

The active use of ICT technology for quarantine was possible through the cooperation of not only medical institutions but also various entities such as financial services, police, telecommunications companies, and local governments. In the case of a confirmed case, it was possible to quickly identify the confirmed person's travel route using credit card company information, and by establishing a system that notifies close contacts by text message via telecommunications company. Such measures greatly contributed to preventing the initial spread of COVID-19. In addition, it was able to play a role in greatly reducing the burden of the government's quarantine manpower and resources. Moreover, as the government's quarantine activities were communicated to citizens then and there, transparency and reliability of the government's quarantine policies were also increased.

The quarantine system using ICT has opened up the possibility of significant personal information infringement. China adopted the health code in Shenzhen on February 9, 2020, when COVID-19 started to spread rapidly. From that point forward, the app, used by each local government in China, has been able to access the user's travel history, residence, and medical records. Using this information, the individual's risk level could be expressed in red, yellow, and green, and most people used Alipay and WeChat as platforms. Since it was possible to access not only personal movement but also health-related information, the possibility of extensive personal information infringement became raised. Singapore similarly launched an app called TraceTogether on March 20, 2020. People who installed this app allowed the government to quarantine using this information if the contact was found to be a confirmed case after the mobile phone saved information on nearby people who had close contact with each other. This app, which used a technology called Blue Trace, deleted information after a certain period of time and made it impossible for individuals to know who they have been in contact with, but it is a serious privacy violation because the government can identify not only the individual's movement route but also who is the person he or she has been in contact with.

In the case of Korea, contacts were tracked using mobile phone location tracking and credit card usage information. In the case of Trace Together, individuals voluntarily installed the app, but in Korea, mobile phone location tracking or credit card information are able to be used without personal consent. This was allowed by the Infectious Disease Prevention Act after the MERS outbreak in 2015, but the risk of personal information infringement was very high. The biggest problem in Korea was that among the collected information, a lot of personal information unrelated to infectious disease prevention was disclosed in the early stage.

The civil society played a significant role in raising the issue of privacy and the protection of minority groups. In February 2020, the Korean government started to use a short message service (SMS) and the internet to share information. During the MERS crisis, the government did not share the details of patients and hospital information, which aggravated fake news. To resolve this problem, the Korean government established the Office of Risk Communication to provide guidelines about how to share information promptly. While the office of risk communication tried to minimize the privacy violation, the government publicized the patient's age, gender, and workplace name. However, the government did not give any justification as to why such information was necessary for effective response to COVID-19 at the expense of the privacy of citizens. Facing the growing risk of the privacy problem, civil rights movement groups protested against the government. As a result, on March 14, 2020, the National Human Rights Commission of Korea admitted the problem and revised the information disclosure guideline not to open age, gender, detailed address, and the workplace name of the infected.

Response to infectious disease using ICTs can increase efficiency to a certain extent, but it cannot solve the problem altogether. As a matter of fact, the process of triaging, testing, and isolating those who have been traced and close contacts requires significant manpower and resources. In the case of an explosive increase in the number of confirmed cases, no matter how quickly close contacts are identified, using ICT is not possible. It is inevitably difficult to manage because inspection or quarantine facilities are not properly equipped. Therefore, although a close contact tracing system using ICT can be useful in the early stage of confirmation, citizens do not voluntarily use the system for the fear of personal information infringement, resulting in a decrease in the efficiency of the system. In reality, many countries claimed that strong ICT-based tracing and monitoring policies would effectively control the spread of COVID-19, but it turned out that most of these efforts failed and went through several re-proliferation processes. It can be argued that ICT has increased the efficiency of the COVID-19 response in various ways. However, since there is a possibility that the result of the efficiency may have been overestimated, it is necessary to sufficiently evaluate its effectiveness in the aftermath of it all. In the case of Korea, various apps for QR checks or body temperature monitoring were used, but none of them have been properly evaluated. This is because citizens' voluntary quarantine efforts are likely to be more effective than individual behavior control through technology. Active use of ICT is suggested as a reason for Korea's successful response to COVID-19, but this is only part of the success factor. It is worth remembering that the risk of unintended consequences due to privacy infringement and excessive disclosure of data by the government could have been a substantial factor. This is because excessive trust in information technology can be misused and overestimated. It could indeed be misused to justify the collection of information about citizens by the government in the post-COVID-19 world.

In this respect, it is noteworthy that each country has established guidelines on government collection and disclosure and has attempted to comply with them in order to prevent infringement of personal information. Europe Data Protection Board issued the "Guidelines 04/2020 on the use of location data and contact tracing tools in the context of the COVID-19 outbreak" in April 2020. According to this guideline,

> contact tracing applications must be voluntary, serve the purpose of managing the COVID-19 health crisis only, respect the principle of data minimization, and ask for the data subjects' consent to any operations that are not strictly necessary. Special attention should be paid to the regular review of algorithms and to applying state-of-the-art cryptographic techniques to secure the stored data. Finally, reporting users as infected with COVID-19 on the application must be subject to proper authorization.[13]

In the case of Korea, the National Human Rights Commission of Korea also expressed concern regarding personal information infringement on March 9, 2020, but it was only on October 7, 2020, that the Central Defense Countermeasure Headquarters issued 'Guidelines for Disclosure of Information' such as movement route of confirmed patients (first edition). Even in these guidelines, it was not sufficiently explained on what principles information should be disclosed and how disclosed information can contribute to preventing proliferation. This is a problem that arose because there was a situation that emphasized quarantine efficiency rather than personal information protection in exceptional circumstances such as COVID-19, which has a strong personal information protection law.

Since the world has already conducted activities to respond to COVID-19 using various forms of ICT, in the post-COVID-19 world, it is necessary to improve guidelines that can increase quarantine efficiency while minimizing the side effects of ICT based on each country's COVID-19 experience.

## 5.4 Public–Private Collaboration in COVID-19 Testing and Treatment

The role of the government is very important when it comes to a disaster response process, but it is important to remember that various technologies and medical facilities are also needed to respond to COVID-19. The problem is that the government cannot provide these technologies and medical facilities alone, but requires proactive collaboration from private hospitals and pharmaceutical companies. The same applies to disaster relief payments. Even if disaster subsidies are paid to those who have suffered economic damage due to COVID-19, it is common to pay them through credit card companies or private financial systems rather than directly by the government. Therefore, cooperation between the public sector and the private sector is essential.

In general, public–private partnerships are often led by the government. However, a representative case in which the private sector has played an active role in the COVID-19 response process is the development of a mask app. The mask app was possible under Korea's unique national public health insurance system.

Korea has the National Health Insurance (NHI) system in which all Korean and qualified foreigners can use and benefit from the universal health care service. Before the implementation of the National Health Insurance Act in 2000, there were three independent medical insurance systems: regional insurance, government employee insurance, and private school teacher and employee insurance. Such independent insurance systems turned out to be inefficient, and there was deepening inequality among insurance systems. The NHI system not only reduced operating costs by integrating these three medical insurance systems, but also built an integrated information management system in the NHIS that could pass information independently collected from each medical insurance system.[14] As a result, while private hospitals account for 94.3% of all hospitals in Korea, medical services are well coordinated through the NHI system equipped with a well-established database system.

In addition to this, Korea established a system of separation of prescribing and dispensing, and dualized hospitals to prescribe and pharmacies to provide prescribed drugs. Korea's medical insurance system is as follows. First, NHIS collects medical insurance premiums by requiring all citizens to subscribe to medical insurance. Medical insurance premiums collected in this way are provided to institutions that provide medical services, such as hospitals and pharmacies. HIRA reviews health care providers' bills to see if they are appropriate NHIS with this review, which NHIS pays for.

And all these processes are monitored and managed by the Ministry of Health and Welfare. The amount of information produced in this process is staggering. Each year, 1.3 billion claims are made by 100,000 hospitals and pharmacies, and 51 million people receive health insurance services. This information was managed by independent data platforms of HIRA and NHIS prior to COVID-19 (Figure 5.9).

Information sharing between HIRA and NHIS occurred during the government's mask supply process in the midst of responding to COVID-19. In February 2020, as the mask shortage became serious due to the increase in confirmed cases, the government announced a policy to directly supply masks.

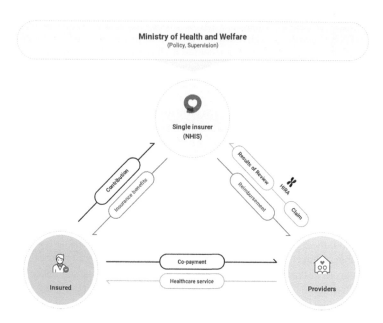

*Figure 5.9* National health insurance system and actors. Ministry of Health and Welfare (Policy, Supervision). *Source:* National Health Insurance Service.

In order for the government to supply masks, it was necessary to purchase masks from producers and supply them to pharmacies, but it was also necessary to prevent duplicate purchases, manage vendors, and manage appropriate inventory. At the time, the government had to quickly build an information system related to mask supply to ensure transparent supply of masks. In the case of using various health insurance-related apps that were previously operated by the government, service overload problems occurred when multiple users accessed the system all at once, and user convenience was also reduced. However, there was a problem that took a considerable amount of time in the development and dissemination stages (Figure 5.10).

Civilian experts played a significant role in developing a variety of platforms for sharing information about mask availability and the infection and fatality cases. There was a significant mask shortage problem toward the end of February 2020 and the government announced that it fully controlled face mask distribution on March 5, 2020. Despite the announcement, citizens did not have information about the availability of masks in the pharmacies. However, a 'civic hacking group' composed of ordinary citizens requested the opening of public data on the government's public bulletin board and also proposed the development of a mask app. Accordingly, citizen developers

| 1.  Utilize existing public health apps | 2.  Develop a new app | 3.  Seek public–private partnerships |
|---|---|---|
| • Disseminate mask-related information through existing apps such as "Health Information" app provided by Health Insurance Review & Assessment Service and "Emergency Medical Information" app of the Ministry of Health and Welfare (Central Emergency Medical Center). | • The government entrusts the private App developers for the app development. | • The government provides the data on the sales of public mask.<br>• Private App developers willfully develop the relevant apps. |
| • Need to unify pharmacy codes on the aforementioned two apps.<br>• Disruptions due to excessive web traffic may occur. | • Time to prepare is needed before launching the app and high construction cost.<br>• Government procurement process needs a certain period of time (approx. a month)<br>• Excessive web traffic may lead to app malfunctions. | • Swift provision of high-quality information is possible thanks to the private sector.<br>• Need to convert the data to the publicly available form.<br>• Separate API server is needed. |

source : The Ministry of Science and ICT(2020)

*Figure 5.10* Three ways to develop public mask applications (apps) for COVID-19.
*Source:* The Ministry of Science and ICT (2020).

and government officials gathered together to check the development potential, and HIRA, NIA (Korea Intelligent Information Society Agency), cloud companies (KT, Koscom, NHN, NBP), citizen developer groups, and web app development companies. A task force was formed and development started. What can be seen is that many actors were involved in the process of developing a mask app. HIRA utilized existing pharmacy and other medical facility management information to provide mask vendor name, address, warehousing quantity, sales quantity, and inventory information. NIA processed mask data and disclosed it to private developers through an Open API method. They used this information to quickly create an app program. Additionally, cloud companies provided cloud infrastructure so that private developers' app could use cloud service free of charge. As a result, on March 11, five days after the task force was created, the mask app was officially released and started to be used. During this development process and actual use process, government and private experts communicated through online spaces and citizens continued to provide feedback, which meant that the app could be rapidly stabilized. This mask app made citizens believe that the government transparency was the force behind supplying masks, and despite the government's mask supply control, mask purchases were made without major confusion.

Another successful example of public–private partnership was the development of a COVID-19 test kit. In a situation where vaccines and effective treatments were not well developed in January 2020, the most effective response was to reduce the spread of infection and quickly treat patients to relieve symptoms. Rapid testing was a key means of reducing the spread of infection. When the COVID-19 virus first started to spread, the test kits were not yet fully developed. For the testing to be effective, it was necessary to (1) secure accurate and prompt test kits, (2) secure medical institutions that can conduct tests, and (3) promptly notify test results and isolate confirmed patients.

On January 10, the researchers from Fudan University released the gene sequencing data of the isolated 2019-nCoV, and the KCDC analyzed the information. On January 11, 2020, the KCDC announced that it will develop a better new test method than the pan-coronavirus method which takes around two days to get the test results. Despite the announcement of the KCDC, few believed that the Korean government could develop the new test method within a month as it announced.

Even when the government announced that it would develop a COVID-19 diagnostic kit, it was unknown whether COVID-19 would grow into a global pandemic. During this time, private companies showed strategic agility and quickly embarked on the development of COVID-19 diagnostic kits. This was a very risky decision for a private company to develop such kits. If it were a general situation, it would have taken a year and a half from the submission of the necessary documents to getting approval by the Korean government. The Korean government announced the speeding up of the process to approve of the COVID-19 test kit. At that time, the Korean Society of Laboratory Medicine formed a COVID-19 response task force and proposed to the government to use the PCR method proposed by WHO as a standard. Private companies also began to rush the development of the PCR method. The development of diagnostic kits was accelerated due to private companies implementing their technological innovations, such as analyzing genetic information using super computers rather than developing diagnostic kits by directly analyzing the COVID-19 in the laboratory. As a result, a private company called KogeneBiotech developed the first test kit and got approval on February 4, 2020. It was three weeks after the release of the COVID-19 genetic sequence on January 10, 2020. Four other companies also developed their test kits and got swift emergency approval from the government. Notably, all these companies are small- and medium-sized enterprises. The new test kit reduced the test time from one to two days to 6 hours, later shortened to 20 minutes.

From January 30, 18 research institutes of public health and environment in each local government were permitted to conduct tests, and from February 7, tests were expanded to private medical institutions also. Due to such efforts, in February 2020, Korea was able to effectively control the initial spread through rapid and extensive COVID-19 testing.

Efforts in public–private partnership were also prominent in the process of extensive COVID-19 testing and vaccination since then. The comprehensive test was launched and the government performed more than 13,000 tests a week later (February 26, 2020) of the outbreak in Daegu. Later on, the number of tests reached 18,199 per day at its peak, on its top. The number is remarkable given that few countries had enough test kits and skills at that time as Korea did. Also, while the number of new infection cases had significantly dropped since mid-March, the number of tests was still as high as around 10,000 per day until early April 2020. Such extensive COVID-19 testing was not possible with government-run public hospitals or public health centers. Temporary screening inspection centers were quickly established in parks, public parking lots, and gymnasiums, and many volunteers, doctors, and nurses supported inspection work at the temporary screening centers.

Some doctors suggested drive-through testing to minimize contact during the COVID-19 examination process, providing an idea for rapid testing. In addition, not only the government but also private internet companies quickly provided places where COVID-19 testing and vaccination were possible online.

Active cooperation between the government and the private sector was also carried out in the stages of installing quarantine facilities and securing medical personnel. As medical facilities could not be secured in a short period of time, it was difficult to secure facilities to isolate confirmed cases and close contacts. In the early stages of the spread of COVID-19, private companies were allowed to use training centers as facilities for quarantine for those who were in close contact with confirmed cases. Additionally, since the degree of COVID-19 spread widely by region, local governments that had room for medical facilities and manpower provided medical personnel and facilities to local governments with severe spread. Volunteers carried out activities in various fields, such as making masks, supporting COVID-19 inspection activities, distributing quarantine items, quarantine and income, and supporting households vulnerable to COVID-19.

To avoid excessive amounts of people gathering to get the vaccine, priority targets were selected so that they could be vaccinated at public health centers or private hospitals. Individual vaccination information was officially verified through the blockchain-based COVID-19 Vaccination Verification System (COOV) developed through collaboration with a private blockchain company. In addition, vaccination information was also provided to private internet portal companies such as Kakao, and was used for restaurants and various multiunit facilities requiring vaccination.

Finally, the Korean government organized the recovery committee to discuss how to prepare for the post-covid era in October 2021. The committee, chaired by the prime minister, consisted of many subcommittees, with 31 civilian representatives from businesses, hospitals, academia, culture and sports, and local governments. These representatives actively expressed their concerns and suggested ideas to the recovery committee. Such involvement of citizens in the recovery committee helped the government design COVID-19 response policies.

Regarding the role of the public and private sectors, there is a controversy that the quality and quantity of public hospitals matter when it comes to pandemic situations. In Korea, discussions concerning the expansion of public health care institutions surfaced during the MERS. The director of Incheon Metropolitan City Medical Center, Seong Yeon Cho, argued that a lack of public health institutions led to the loss of defense against national catastrophic diseases (such as SARs, swine flu, and MERS), and stated that public health care should be strengthened, the United Kingdom being cited as an example. With the COVID-19 crisis emerging, the argument for the expansion of public health care institutions once again re-surfaced. Jae Joon Jang, a research fellow at the Korea Institute for Health and Social Affairs, claimed that despite the oversupply of hospital bed resources in Korea, as COVID-19 started to rapidly spread, hospitalization became difficult due to a lack of wards. He argued that the reasons for the COVID-19-related deaths were lack of hospital beds and hospital resources in public medical institutions. According to the OECD, the total number of hospitals in Korea amounts to 3,924 (94.3%) and the number of public health care institutions is 224 (5.7%), confirming that the number of public health care institutions is overwhelmingly low. However, it is difficult to argue that the number of public health institutions leads to an improvement in the quality of response to infectious diseases. Regardless of ownership, in the case of a national catastrophic infectious disease, private hospitals are also subject to be under the control of the Ministry of Health and Welfare in accordance with the Emergency Medical Service Act. As shown Figure 5.7, Iceland, the United Kingdom, and Slovenia have more than 90% of public hospitals, but there is no evidence that they can effectively reduce the confirmed cases of COVID-19 (Figure 5.11).

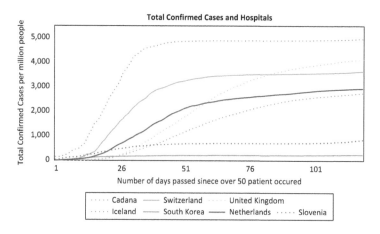

*Figure 5.11* The cumulative number of confirmed cases in countries with more than 90% of private and public medical institutions. *Source:* Organization for Economic Cooperation and Development (OECD); European Center for Disease Control and Prevention (ECDC); John Hopkins University (JHU).

## 5.5 Social Distancing Policies and Citizens' Compliance

In the latter half of the 20th century, the international community succeeded in establishing a global system of cooperation based on free international trade and movement. This system effectively connected nations and facilitated the creation of a global value chain that promised to eradicate poverty and achieve common prosperity in the 21st century. In furtherance of this goal, European countries embraced the Schengen Agreement, which aimed to minimize restrictions on cross-border traffic by establishing a common concept of borders. However, the global COVID-19 crisis, which emerged in the early 21st century, has upended this system and forced the world to adopt a global social distancing policy that is unprecedented in human history. The social distancing policy aimed at reducing or slowing the spread of infectious diseases by minimizing physical contact between people implemented at individual, community, or governmental levels. The most representative policies include physical distancing, shelter-in-place, closure of non-essential businesses, limiting gatherings, remote work, etc. While social distancing policies are assumed successful in mitigating the spread of the virus, it remains to be seen whether they provide valuable lessons for disaster management. This is a matter that requires further consideration and analysis.

In response to the COVID-19 pandemic that originated in Wuhan, China, in December 2019, numerous countries have implemented extraordinary measures to prevent and mitigate the spread of infections and deaths. Among them, the most notable authoritarian measure was China's decision to impose a lockdown on the city of Wuhan. On January 23, 2020, the Chinese government declared that no one could leave Wuhan City, and after two weeks of the lockdown, 14 provinces in China implemented lockdown or similar policies. Approximately 41 countries denied entry to anyone who had been in China as of February 20, 2020. While some countries initially criticized such draconian policies that limited individual travel rights, the travel ban has become a standard policy in other countries following the pandemic's spread in Europe, the United States, and elsewhere. As of the end of March 2020, most countries had adopted partial or complete bans on international and/or domestic travel. For instance, 145 countries banned the entry of travelers arriving from Korea, and 51 countries partially banned travelers from high-risk cities such as Daegu or enforced quarantine on recent arrivals from Korea in March 2020.

The question arises as to why the travel ban has become so popular and regarded as the global standard. First, it is a politically acceptable measure. The influx of infectious diseases from other countries has a similar psychological effect as a physical invasion from foreign countries, leading to the public opinion that foreigners should be banned from entering the nation. While xenophobia already existed in Europe and the United States before the COVID-19 outbreak, the pandemic reinforced hatred toward certain races and nationalities. Second, the travel ban is easy for the government to implement. Regardless of the costs, the government can impose international travel bans simply by arguing that there is an urgent need to protect its citizens. Third, as social contact is believed to be a direct cause of infection, travel bans are intuitively appealing, as fewer contacts result in fewer infections. However, the director-general of the WHO argued that "travel restrictions can cause more harm than good by hindering info-sharing, medical supply chains, and harming economies" (BBC News, 3 February 2020).

As one of the social distancing measures, the travel ban has been supported by biological and epidemiological rationale for a long time. Social distancing measures usually consist of both domestic and international measures to curtail the spread of pandemics, including isolating infected persons, contact-tracing methods, quarantining exposed persons, school dismissals or closures, workplace measures such as work-from-home policies, avoiding crowding, air travel bans, and immigration bans. Given the increased connectivity of global society, travel bans have become both domestic and international issues affecting global citizens.

The effectiveness of travel bans in controlling the spread of pandemics is a topic of ongoing debate, with empirical evidence showing inconsistent results. Brownstein et al. (2006) conducted a study to examine the influence of international air travel on the spread of influenza in the United States. Their analysis compared the period before and after September 11, 2001, when there was a significant drop in airline traffic volume. The authors suggest that a reduction in airline traffic leads to a decrease in the domestic spread of influenza. While they caution against drawing a positive relationship between air travel volume and global spread of the virus, they also argue that travel bans can be an effective policy tool in controlling influenza.

In a more recent study, Tian et al. (2020) found a strong positive correlation between the number of travels from Wuhan to other cities in China and the cumulative number of COVID-19 cases before January 30. Similarly, Kraemer et al. (2020) suggest that China's restriction on movement had a significant impact on preventing the spread of COVID-19 within China. However, Chinazzi et al. (2020) noted that the movement restrictions in China only delayed the spread of COVID-19 by a few days due to the large number of people who had already left Wuhan before the control measures were put in place.

Cooper et al. (2006) challenge the effectiveness of the air travel restriction on curbing the spread of the pandemic. The transmission of the influenza virus is so quick that the travel ban is ineffective unless all travelers are stopped the moment the outbreak is detected in a city. When the infection rate is high, multiple strategies (both social and medical interventions) are required to contain the spread (Germann et al., 2006). Another study on the 2009 H1N1 pandemic (Bajadi et al., 2011) showed that Mexico's air travel was reduced by 40%, but this measure delayed the spread of the virus for only about three days. Gostin and Lucey (2015) insisted that travel restrictions were not effective in 2015 for MERS (Middle East respiratory syndrome coronavirus, MERS-CoV) due to lack of community transmission.

The feasibility of implementing travel bans also undermines the effectiveness of the policy. As Fraser et al. (2004) suggest, it is difficult to gauge the extent of control if the pandemic has mild or no symptoms. Temperature screening of international travelers is not effective in detecting infected persons when only mild symptoms or asymptomatic patients are considerably present. As a result, regardless of visible symptoms, all travelers from high-risk countries have to be quarantined. This incurs huge costs for both travelers and hosting countries. Fong et al. (2020) reviewed the effectiveness of six domestic social distancing measures and concluded that they indeed reduced transmission and delayed the time taken for the total cases to reach its peak. In their review, the effectiveness of social distancing measures depends on the reproduction rate of diseases ($R_0$), degree of policy mixes, and compliance of citizens to social distancing measures. Despite the debates about the effectiveness of travel bans, most countries adopted different levels of travel bans at different stages of COVID-19 spread.

Because of the absence of vaccines and treatment drugs for COVID-19, social distancing policies have become more critical than before. Right after China began to admit the spread of COVID-19, Korean society debated the option of banning travelers from China. The KCDC was aware of the potential risk of COVID-19; it installed thermal scanners at airports to detect suspicious patients from China on January 3, 2020. However, when the first confirmed patient, a Chinese from Wuhan, was officially announced on January 20, many Koreans called for closing the borders to Chinese travelers. Initially, this seemed to be the best solution, but the Korean government did not close the border; instead, it reinforced the entry-point quarantine.

Moreover, the Korean government did not impose a lockdown on cities or ban citizens' travel. Public transportation, such as buses, taxis, and subways, was operated under the official control measures of COVID-19. This measure prevented massive layoffs and negative impacts, especially on the low-income group that originated from mobility restrictions. Despite initially pursuing liberal disaster response policies, Korea was gradually forced to adopt social distancing policies adopted by other countries as the WHO declared a pandemic in March 2020.

Initially, the government did not use the term 'social distancing policy'. Instead, the government issued response policies such as school closing, enforcement of working from home, and prevention of social gatherings. Interestingly, while there were only around 400 infection cases per day, the Korean government issued social distancing policies that suspended the operation of religious facilities, some types of indoor sports facilities (dancing halls, health clubs, martial arts training centers), and entertainment facilities (entertainment bars, clubs, karaoke rooms) on March 22, 2020. At the time, the government wanted to control COVID-19 cases at a zero level and there was no idea about 'tolerable infection level'. It resulted in the successive extension of social distancing policies. Even in March 2020, the Korean government had no intention of continuing its social distancing policy for long.

The social distancing policies were planned only for two weeks, but they were extended for an additional two weeks on April 7, 2020. The justification for the extension was that there were still around 100 new infection cases, which was minor compared to other countries. At the time, the recognition of the occurrence of 100 daily cases of infection as a very serious situation was due to the fear of the high transmissibility of the coronavirus. Additionally, the government's decision to prioritize political considerations to avoid responsibility for the failure of epidemic control, despite the occurrence of manageable levels of infections, also played a role. This was compounded by the strengthened social distancing policies implemented by other countries, which created pressure for the government to demonstrate strong leadership in epidemic control. The effects of the government's avoidance of political responsibility and its pursuit of a strong epidemic control leadership were evident in the policies of some local governments. In May 2020, the Seoul Metropolitan government strongly prohibited opening entertainment facilities because of the community infection found in the nightclubs of Itaewon. However, the number of infection cases per day was less than 50. While such social distancing policies perhaps reduced infection numbers and reduced political responsibility, this came at a hefty price for businessmen.

Originally, the social distancing policy aimed at 'flattening the curve', which slowed down the rapid spread, rather than aiming for perfect quarantine. However, as social distancing policies began to be universally adopted in other countries, Korea also switched to maintaining social distancing policies. A rational judgment process was needed on what goal and level to set the level of social distancing policy, but the government failed to present an active explanation to citizens. In particular, although the policy target variable should gradually change from reducing the number of confirmed cases to lowering the fatality rate, the social distancing policy was mainly focused on reducing the number of confirmed cases.

The social distancing policy not only has a very high social cost, but also has a high possibility of violating individual freedom and greatly damaging social solidarity. Even the decline in the quality of education and the decline in social skills that occur when students do not go to school cause significant social losses in the long run and even lead to a rapid economic downturn. Nonetheless, bureaucrats prefer this policy because the costs of social distancing are spread across the majority of citizens rather than being concentrated on the government. In many cases, it is difficult to respond to the bureaucracy accustomed to institutional inertia to create a new response policy in a crisis situation, so policies with high administrative costs within the bureaucracy are not preferred. In addition, social distancing policies are not politically favored in everyday situations because of the high political burden, but in the case of a pandemic, strong leadership is often preferred. In particular, it can be understood that the fear of the pandemic justifies the social distancing policy with the logic of community protection and national security. For this reason, paradoxically, strong social distancing policies are preferred rather than persuading citizens and demanding voluntary quarantine efforts.

In fact, while implementing the social distancing policy, Korea did not present specific standards and scientific grounds, so the predictability of the policy was considerably lowered. A systematic social distancing policy guideline was introduced on June 28, 2020, in Korea. At the time, as shown in Table 5.3, the social distancing policy was designed into three levels according to the number of infection cases. Level 3 was designed to be issued when the two-week average daily confirmed cases exceeded 100. The criteria,

*Table 5.3* Three-level social distancing policy (from June 28)

| | Level 1 | Level 2 | Level 3 (lockdown) |
|---|---|---|---|
| Daily community infection for two weeks | Less than 50 people | 50 to less than 100 people | 100–200 people or more |
| Key message | Comply with quarantine rules and permit daily economic activities | Avoid unnecessary outings and use of multipurpose facilities | All activities other than essential economic activities are prohibited |
| Gathering | Allowed (recommended to comply with quarantine rules) | 50 people indoors, no more than 100 people outdoors | No more than 10 people |
| Sports event | Limit the number of spectators | No spectators | Stop all sports events |
| Public facilities | Allowed (with interventions if necessary) | Shutdown | Shutdown |
| School | School attendance and remote classes | Reduction of school attendance and remote classes | Remote classes or closure of the school |
| Workplace | Flextime and work from home | More flextime and work from home | Except for essential personnel, all public employees are to work from home |

*Source:* The Ministry of Health and Welfare (MOHW).

however, were criticized to have been proposed without any scientific explanation and considered too restrictive. The effectiveness of the school closing policy has never been scientifically tested. Instead, the government asked citizens to reduce mobility and physical contact.

The three-tier social distancing policy was revised on November 7, 2020, as the number of infection cases rapidly increased. In the revision, levels 1 and 2 were divided into four levels (1, 1.5, 2, and 2.5), and level 3 was made to be issued when new cases were more than 800. Furthermore, the new guideline considered the hospital capacities, the relative increase of new cases, and regional differences. On December 16, 2020, the level 3 condition was first satisfied as the one-week average new cases were over 800. However, the Korean government did not issue level 3. The decision was because of the serious negative impact of the lockdown on the economy. The Korean government's experiences and outcomes reveal that the decision to raise the social distancing policy level is not an easy task and can vary according to regional, political, and economic situations.

The social distancing policy is not necessarily strongly correlated with the trend of new confirmed cases. As shown in Figure 5.12, the level of social distancing policies such as workplace closing and canceling public events have changed over time. The changes in the level do not necessarily reflect the severity of infection cases. For instance, the daily new cases were relatively small during April and June 2020, but the Korean government maintained a high social distancing policy. Also, the level of public event regulation changes more frequently compared to workplace closing.

Despite the merits of incremental and flexible social distancing policy changes, decision-making related to the right time for and the right level of social distancing policy is very challenging. For instance, although the government allowed restaurants to open their business, the health clubs were asked to close under level 2.5 of the social distancing policy. The government failed to explain why health clubs are riskier than restaurants.

The success or failure of disaster response does not originate from a single actor if we assume that the disaster response network is a complex system (Perrow, 1984). The disaster management cycle consisting of preparedness, response, recovery, and mitigation involves multiple actors and different types of interactions at different stages of the cycle. Due to the nature of coupled and dynamic systems, civil society's role becomes more critical than social distancing policy.

Instead of relying on a forceful social distancing policy, the Korean society benefits from citizens' voluntary quarantine and hygiene efforts. When the Korean government adopted a strict quarantine policy between February 19 and July 10, 2020, there were 324,160 self-quarantined people in Korea. Among them, only 0.16% of them failed to comply with the self-quarantine policy. Even when the violation occurred, citizens reported the violation

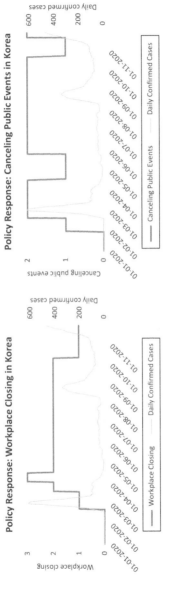

*Figure 5.12* Workplace closing and canceling public events intensity. *Source:* Our World in Data.

cases. Contrary to the argument that the government should impose a strong penalty to noncompliance, there is no evidence that it reduced noncompliance. As shown in Figure 5.13, while the Korean government adopted the one-strike-out policy and increased the amount of violation penalty on April 5, 2000, there is no evidence that there is a significant reduction in violation cases (Ryu et al., 2022).

Despite the multiple unexpected waves of COVID-19, there was no panic buying in Korea. Even in February and March 2020, when the supply of masks was very low, a certain amount was calmly purchased according to the government's public mask policy. In addition, there was no great confusion because vaccination was performed according to the priority presented by the government during vaccination. There was also no significant difference in daily mobility activities. The interregional express traffic dropped to 60.2% in the first week of April 2020 compared to that of the third week of January (KOTI, 2020). However, highway traffic only decreased by –3.3% in the same period. This implies that citizens avoided public transportation to avoid contact with others and decided to use their cars to travel between regions. Within the city, people used their cars, bicycles, and other forms of mobility. Such behavioral changes suggest that citizens were able to find better solutions for resolving the inconveniences in their daily life caused by COVID-19. Such a choice was not enforced by the government but resulted from creative problem-solving efforts by the citizens.

Figure 5.14 shows the mobility change of the Seoul metropolitan region and the nation. Also, the step function shows the social distance policy level. The largest number of infection cases in Korea was on March 1, 2020, and the mobility to transit and retail showed the lowest level. At the time, however, the government's social distance policy remained at level 1. This suggests that the reduction of mobility is not because of the regulation of the government. Instead, citizens voluntarily reduced their mobility regardless of the government's enforcement.

It is also worth noting that the intensity of social distancing in Korea was relatively low compared to other countries. Figure 5.15 compares the trends of

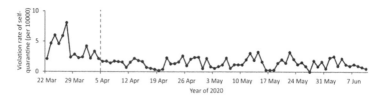

*Figure 5.13* The violation rate of self-quarantine per 10,000. *Source:* Ryu et al. (2022: 466).

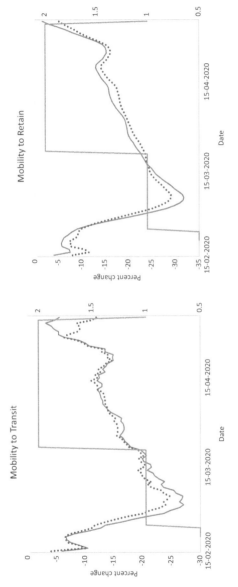

*Figure 5.14* Mobility change and social distancing policy. *Note:* The dashed line is for the Seoul Metropolitan and the Solid line is for the national level trend. The step line is about the social distancing policy level. *Source:* Our World in Data, COVID-19 Community Mobility Reports, Google.

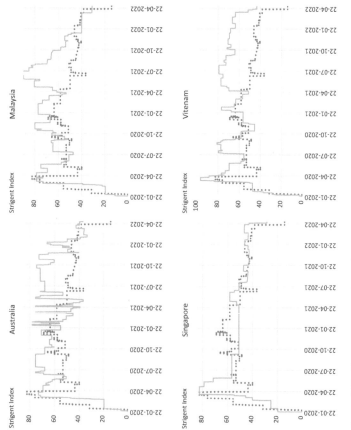

*Figure 5.15* The government stringent index of Asian countries compared to Korea. *Note:* Dashed line is the trend of Korea. *Source:* Our World in Data.

the Government Response Stringent Index provided by Oxford's Our World in Data (OWID) at the University of Oxford. Looking at this, it can be seen that overall the intensity of social distancing policies in Korea was low compared to other countries and was at a similar level to Singapore.

The fact that Korea carried out quarantine based on the relative autonomy of its citizens is revealed well in the mobility trend analysis. Compared to Singapore and Thailand, which are known to have successfully carried out epidemic prevention and control in Asia, Korea's mobility reduction trend is indeed impressive. In Figure 5.16, the reference point represents the number of visitors to transit stations from January 3, 2000, to February 6, 2020. In Singapore and Thailand, there was a more than 60% drop in mobility during April 2020. On the contrary, Korea rarely dropped its mobility level below –30%. This implies that the Korean social distancing policy is implemented not threatening the normal life of citizens.

Even in the early days of COVID-19, it was thought that the spread of the disease could have been prevented by social distancing policies, but from the results of the spread of COVID-19 from 2020 to 2023, this has proven to not have been the case. Above all, a critical review is necessary in that the social distancing policy basically limited numerous basic rights, such as the right to learn, the right to move, the right to do business, freedom of assembly, and freedom of residence, in the name of public health.

Modern society is characterized by a very close connection, among individuals, organizations, and various functions. The social distancing policy resulted in a great shock to the world, and the world seemed to have transitioned into a hyper-connected society. Social distancing should not lead to personal isolation or curtail various forms of social interaction. This is because in a fragmented society, it is challenging to solve problems caused by COVID-19 together. Therefore, while implementing social distancing policies, adverse effects of the state's control or reduction of social networks should be minimized. Instead, there is a need to find solutions to problems through a social network, share them, and overcome COVID-19 through mutual cooperation. In this regard, it is necessary to increase the degree of compliance with the social distancing policy based on citizen autonomy. What is noteworthy among Korea's experiences is that citizens were able to respond to infectious diseases without significantly reducing their mobility while also maintaining their daily lives. It is important to learn the lesson that if the social distancing policy is strongly enforced while undermining the autonomy of civil society, it can reduce the resilience and responsiveness of society compared to the effectiveness of quarantine.

On the other hand, it is worth noting that the social distancing policy has great institutional rigidity. In fact, in 2022, as the vaccination rate increased and Omicron mutation revealed a low fatality rate, the demand to abolish the PCR test policy for wearing outdoor masks or entering and exiting the country became stronger. However, fearing responsibility for the re-proliferation of

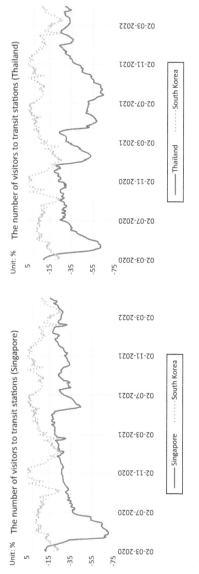

*Figure 5.16* Trend of mobility to transit station (Singapore and Thailand compared to Korea). *Source:* COVID-19 Community Mobility Reports, Google.

COVID-19, some public officials and policymakers tended to maintain the existing social distancing policy. In a situation where other OECD countries have already abolished most of the PCR test obligations upon entry, Korea required all arrivals to undergo PCR testing within one day by October 1, 2022. Additionally, wearing masks outdoors was made optional on September 26, 2022, and the need to wear masks indoors was lifted on January 30, 2023. Compared to February 2022, when the United Kingdom completely lifted COVID-related quarantine regulations, including self-isolation, it can be seen that Korean public officials showed very conservative behavior. In particular, the KCDC continued the policy on the grounds that it was necessary for quarantine without providing a scientific basis for the effectiveness of this policy. Consequently, strong resilience from citizens was faced, and it began to expand to criticism of the government's social distancing policy in general. As COVID-19 variants increased, the government encouraged vaccinating with bivariate vaccines, but by the end of December 2022, the vaccination rate was less than 30% for those aged 60 and above. This is a huge difference compared to the 97% of those over 60 who completed the second vaccination. When the government implements the social distancing policy without providing sufficient grounds, the degree of cooperation from the private sector drops sharply, suggesting that such low compliance with the policy can have a negative impact on future disaster response.

Whether or not to adopt social distancing policies is not the most important consideration; rather, finding the appropriate level and timing of such policies is crucial. If the aim of social distancing is solely to eradicate the risk of infection, the most effective measure would be to enforce strict and prolonged social distancing to reduce the risk of transmission to zero. However, the objective of social distancing policies should not be limited to disease prevention alone. It is essential to consider the social and economic impact of such policies and allocate resources appropriately. Therefore, it is necessary to discuss the acceptable level of health risks that society can tolerate while selecting the appropriate level and duration of social distancing measures. If prolonged social distancing policies result in high levels of public fatigue, the costs of the policy will increase sharply, and alternative measures such as individual preventive efforts or sufficient health care services may be more desirable.

Thus, it is highly dangerous to attribute Korea's successful COVID-19 response solely to its strong social distancing policies. Indeed, Korea's low infection and mortality rates can be attributed to a range of factors, including the high rate of mask wearing among citizens, systematic management of close contacts, flexible and effective supply and utilization of private and public health care services, and voluntary prevention efforts based on social solidarity. This suggests that the social distancing policy should be understood as a dynamic policy process that seeks to find the optimal point within the policy network based on the results of social interactions, rather than being based solely on static and authoritarian rationality. The appropriate level of social distancing reached through this dynamic process cannot be identical for all regions and countries, given the flexibility and diversity inherent in disease control strategies. Authoritarian systems have limitations in implementing this approach, as it does not rely on the capacity of civil society to participate in the disaster response policy network, incorporating diverse opinions and possibilities. Therefore, in order to effectively respond to infectious diseases, it is necessary for the government to recognize and utilize the opinions and possibilities of civil society through active engagement. Thus, while social distancing policies may appear to be highly authoritarian, paradoxically, they can be highly effective policies when they are based on the democratic process. This is the lesson that we learn through the COVID-19 response process in Korea.

## 5.6 Fiscal Policy

The emergence of the COVID-19 pandemic resulted in unprecedented government spending across the world. In Korea, the entire cost of COVID-19 diagnostic tests, vaccinations, hospitalization, and isolation of confirmed patients was borne by the government rather than the individuals. To alleviate the financial burden of individuals during the isolation period, the government also provided living support expenses. Also, government financial expenditures were directed toward securing hospitals and medical facilities for the treatment of COVID-19 patients. Besides such expenditure related to public health and medical services, the Korean government implemented various fiscal policies such as direct cash transfers, wage subsidies, tax relief, business grants and loans, expansion of social programs, and quantitative easing. Although some of these fiscal policies would be controversial in a normal situation, massive budget expenditures and deficits are tolerated by citizens.

Initially, the Korean government focused on providing support to small businesses and industries to address the economic shock caused by the pandemic. However, as the situation continued to worsen, the government gradually expanded its support to include ordinary households. A comprehensive list of the economic stimulus and fiscal support programs announced by the Korean government starting from February 2020 can be found in Table 5.4.

The first financial stimulus package implemented during February 5 to February 12, 2020, was mainly for mitigating impacts on industries, as shown Table 5.5. This package focuses on supply policies that facilitate the supply of quarantine and medical supplies and speed up the customs clearance process of raw materials, and support for small and medium enterprises (SMEs) or micro-businesses that are vulnerable to economic crisis.

The Korean government unveiled its second comprehensive support package in response to the COVID-19 pandemic on February 28, 2020. This was in addition to the first package and amounted to a total of 20 trillion Korean

*Table 5.4* The fiscal policy at the early stage of COVID-19 (February and March, 2020)

| | |
|---|---|
| Feb 5 - Feb 12 | Announced the First "Financial Stimulus Package" |
| Feb 28 | Announced the Second "Financial Support Package" |
| March 16 | Lowered the Base Interest Rate |
| March 17 | Passed Supplementary budget |
| March 18 | Raised Forex Futures trading limits |
| March 19 | Announced the Third "Financial Stimulus Package" |
| | Signed the Currency Swap with the US |
| | Launched the Emergency Economic Council Meeting |
| March 24 | Announced the Fourth "Financial Stimulus Package" |
| March 26 | Announced additional method to Ease FX Market Stability rules |
| | Announced the Supply of Unlimited Liquidity (Korean QE) |
| March 30 | Adopted an Emergency relief payment for the Disaster |

*Source:* The Republic of Korea (March 31, 2020), "Tackling COVID-19: Health, Quarantine and Economic Measures of South Korea", http://kostat.go.kr/file_total/COVID19_5_1.pdf

*Table 5.5* First financial stimulus package (from February 5–12, 2020)

| First financial stimulus package | February 5, 2020 | Second ministerial meeting on economic resilience | Announced the first "Financial Stimulus Package" |
|---|---|---|---|
| | | | Support for supply and demand of sanitary and medical supplies |
| | | | Helping to expedite customs procedures for raw and sub-materials |
| | February 7, 2020 | Third ministerial meeting on economic resilience | Emergency relief fund for affected SMEs (via loans, guarantees, and import and export financing |
| | | | Expanding lending support for micro-business owners (via loans and guarantees) |
| | | | Enhancing monitoring of unfair trading practices in the capital market |
| | February 12, 2020 | Fourth ministerial meeting on economic resilience | Underwriting greater level of accounts receivable insurance and lowering insurance premiums |
| | | | Helping group import and identify alternative procurement countries for raw and sub-materials |
| | | | Enlarging financial support for SMEs and micro-business owners |

*Source:* The Republic of Korea (March 31, 2020), "Tackling COVID-19: Health, Quarantine and Economic Measures of South Korea", http://kostat.go.kr/filetotal/COVID1951.pdf

won in support. In an effort to mitigate the negative effects of the pandemic, the government implemented measures that targeted not only businesses, but also households and local governments.

Moreover, the Central Bank of Korea reduced the base rate from 1.25% to 0.75% on March 16, 2020, and adopted several other measures, such as raising forex futures trading limits, signing currency swaps with other countries to manage foreign exchange rates, and implementing an emergency subsidy for the disaster. One of the main fiscal policy tools employed by the government was the use of supplementary budgets. In Korea, there are two types of budgets: general and supplementary. The former is a regular budget approved by the National Assembly before the fiscal year starts. The latter is designed to address unforeseen events or circumstances that require additional funding beyond what was initially budgeted for. It is typically used to respond to emergencies, such as natural disasters or economic downturns, and includes measures to support the economy and provide relief to affected parties. The supplementary budget is usually passed by the National Assembly in any necessary time. Prior to the COVID-19 pandemic, supplementary budgets in Korea were primarily allocated for job creation and supporting regions affected by industrial crises. These budgets were typically formulated once a year and were not of significant scale. However, during the COVID-19 period, supplementary budgets were formulated four times in 2020 and twice each in 2021 and 2022. Furthermore, these budgets were of much greater scale than before.

The National Assembly passed the first supplementary budget on March 17, 2020, and subsequent budgets were also approved, as shown in Figure 5.17. Notably, the size of the supplementary budget was largest in 2022, despite the fact that COVID-19 fear and social distancing measures were more intense

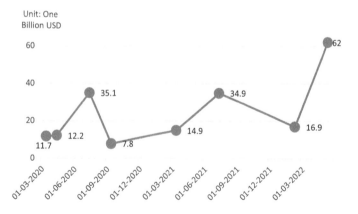

*Figure 5.17* The size of supplementary budgets passed by the national assembly for COVID-19 response. *Source:* Ministry of Economy and Finance.

in 2020 and 2021. This was due to a presidential election that took place on March 9, 2022. Both the ruling and opposition parties promised substantial support to low-income families and merchants affected by COVID-19 in order to gain support in the election. However, criticism arose that the supplementary budget was organized for political purposes and that disaster relief support was provided to citizens.

It is important to evaluate whether the government's expenditures were properly provided to those in need or whether the expenditure targets were well achieved, rather than criticizing that the government's fiscal expenditures were made for political purposes. A similar critique was raised in March 2020 when the first supplementary budget was passed, as neither the ruling nor opposition party could oppose the budget due to the National Assembly election scheduled for April.

During the COVID-19 pandemic, the supplementary budget in Korea played a critical role in supporting medical facilities. Hospitals were hit particularly hard by the pandemic, with many being forced to shut down entirely in the event of any infections. Additionally, the provision of test centers, beds, and special medical facilities to treat COVID-19 patients was extremely costly for medical institutions. Despite the need for quick compensation, the long bureaucratic procedures for payment to hospitals created additional burdens. In response, the Korean government provided rapid compensation for COVID-19 patient treatments using supplementary budgets. Loans were also extended to hospitals and pharmacies struggling with decreased sales.

As the number of confirmed COVID-19 cases surged in November 2020, the need for hospital beds increased. Although Korea had a high number of hospital beds per 1,000 population compared to other OECD countries, the majority of these were located in private hospitals, making it difficult to use them for COVID-19 treatment. Therefore, the government stepped in to provide appropriate compensation and secure the necessary number of COVID beds. As a result, the number of hospital beds steadily increased since 2020. Notably, when the spread of the Omicron mutation led to a significant increase in confirmed cases in 2022, the Korean government ordered private hospitals to secure beds for COVID-19 patients in exchange for financial compensation. This move quickly expanded the number of hospital beds available, enabling the government to reduce the intensity of social distancing policies (Figure 5.18).

At the same time, the Korean government prepared more beds for patients with mild or moderate symptoms, as shown Figure 5.19. Private hospitals supplied the beds, and the government paid the appropriate compensation for them.

The Korean government extended various forms of assistance to households and workers, including support for households in quarantine, employment retention, consumption coupons for low-income households, emergency relief grants, and emergency family care. The most significant challenge in providing this aid was identifying the appropriate beneficiaries. Determining

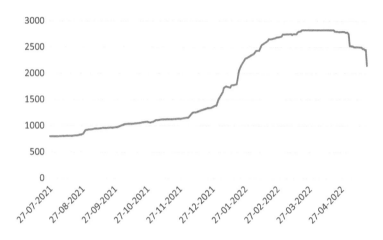

*Figure 5.18* The number of secured intensive care units for COVID-19 patients.

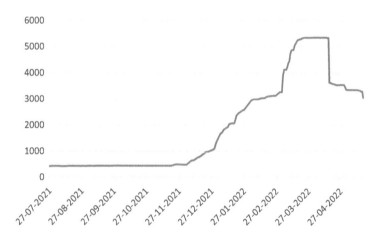

*Figure 5.19* The number of mild or moderate case care units.

the extent of income loss and distinguishing between high asset income and high earned income was difficult, requiring substantial time and administrative costs. This resulted in delays in identifying households severely affected by COVID-19, as well as backlash from those who did not receive assistance. In response, the government decided to pay the first disaster subsidy to all citizens in May 2020 but later changed to selective payment based on income standards unless there was an urgent need.

To support industries, the government provided various measures such as loans, guarantees for business operations, wage and rent support for small merchants, tax cuts, and payment deferrals. Sectors heavily affected by COVID-19, such as tourism, aviation, clothing, and culture and art industries, were unable to survive without government assistance. The local gift certificate system was also instrumental in promoting consumption. Disaster relief funds were distributed as credit cards, local gift certificates, and prepaid cards rather than direct cash. Local gift certificates were issued for use in small businesses in residential areas to revitalize the local economy. Additionally, local love gift certificates were sold at a 10% discount, benefiting local residents and promoting consumption, thereby significantly aiding in the revitalization of the local economy.

Increased fiscal spending to mitigate the impact of COVID-19 on the economy affects the size of government debt. Korea has been following an active fiscal policy centered on welfare spending even before COVID-19. The general government debt as a percentage of GDP (D2) increased by 6.5 percentage points in 2020 compared to 2019, indicating that Korea's expansionary fiscal spending to respond to COVID-19 was relatively modest compared to the United Kingdom (30.52 percentage points) and the United States (25.19 percentage points) (Table 5.6).

The impact of COVID-19 on industries has been subject to an illusion. Although the social distancing policy had a considerable impact on the lodging and food industries, sales of restaurants in Korea decreased only by −3.4% in 2020 and grew by 6.7% in 2021. Additionally, while restaurants faced restrictions such as limiting the number of customers and operating hours, their revenue did not significantly decline due to sales via delivery. Furthermore, Korea did not block cities, resulting in a lesser economic shock. Despite this, the perception that accommodations/restaurants would be severely hit was strong, leading to large-scale government financial support. On the other hand, the arts, sports, and leisure industries faced a relative lack of support despite experiencing an 11.9% decrease in sales in 2020. While economic agents quickly responded to the pandemic's impact, the government had limitations in obtaining rapid statistics to actively address these differences. Thus, budget allocation had to prioritize political burden.

*Table 5.6* Government debt ratio (D2) between 2019 and 2020

| Country | Debt ratio increase (%) |
| --- | --- |
| Korea | 6.8 |
| France | 22.24 |
| Germany | 11.16 |
| USA | 25.19 |
| UK | 30.52 |

*Source:* World Bank

Another illusion to note is the problem of unemployment. While the negative effects of COVID-19 on the economy were expected to lead to a natural increase in unemployment, there was no sharp increase observed in Korea. The trend of the monthly unemployment rate in Figure 5.16 shows that there was no significant increase in the unemployment rate in 2020 compared to 2019, and the unemployment rates have been lowered since April 2021 than in 2019. This indicates that the labor market was relatively stable despite the pandemic. However, the government's support for those who were unemployed via disaster subsidies led to a reduced incentive to return to the labor market, resulting in a job shortage. The unexpected low unemployment rate at the beginning of the COVID-19 pandemic highlights the risk of causing the opposite economic result if the direction of fiscal policy is determined based on common sense without prompt monitoring of changes in the economic situation (Figure 5.20).

The impacts of these policies have been significant. Quantitative easing has helped to boost liquidity in the financial market and support investment and spending. Expansive budget policies have helped to support households, workers, and businesses affected by the pandemic, and prevent the economy from falling into a deeper recession. These policies have also helped to stabilize financial markets and prevent a collapse of the financial system.

However, these policies have also had some negative impacts. Quantitative easing has led to concerns about inflation and potential asset price bubbles. The low interest rates have led to a surge in housing prices, causing young people who do not own homes to strongly resent the government's policy

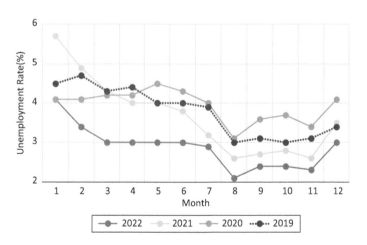

*Figure 5.20* Monthly unemployment rate trend. *Source:* Statistics Korea.

failures. Moreover, the increased liquidity has formed a robust stock market, leading to an increase in investments in speculative virtual assets such as Bitcoin. Expansive budget policies have resulted in a significant increase in government debt, which may pose a risk to fiscal sustainability in the long run. In addition, there have been challenges in identifying appropriate beneficiaries for some of the support measures, and some industries have received more support than others.

Due to the high degree of interconnectedness in modern social systems, fiscal policies aimed at crisis response can have unintended negative consequences. Despite the risk, the active fiscal policy has been repeatedly used in disaster response. The necessity and effectiveness of fiscal policy are emphasized due to the urgency of the disaster situation, but there is a tendency to overlook the various negative effects that it may cause. Interestingly, while some macroeconomic studies have been conducted on the macroeconomic effects of fiscal policy, there is a lack of research on how fiscal policy affects the daily lives of citizens. In such a situation, it is difficult to conduct critical learning, and there is a risk of uncritical implementation of expansionary fiscal policy in repetitive disaster situations. This highlights the need for active evaluations on the potential risks of such fiscal policies implemented after COVID-19 crisis is over.

## Notes

1   Ji, Youngmi (2020), "Public Health Responses to the COVID-19 Outbreak", Korea Institute of Public Administration, Graduate School of Public Administration, Seoul National University.
2   The KCDC has notified Wuhan traveler information to hospitals through the drug utilization review (DUR) since January 9. KCDC Press release. www.cdc.go.kr/board/board.es?mid=a20501000000&bid=0015. January 7.
3   KCDC press release. www.cdc.go.kr/board/board.es?mid=a20501000000&bid=0015. January 16.
4   KCDC press release, www.cdc.go.kr/board/board.es?mid=a20501000000&bid=0015. January 13.
5   http://ncov.mohw.go.kr/
6   https://opengov.seoul.go.kr/seoullove/19932989
7   "Korea Institute of Local Administration (2020), Diagnosis and Challenges of Local Government's Response to Infectious Disease Disasters".
8   The Government of the Republic of Korea (2020), "How Korea Responded to a Pandemic Using ICT: Flattening the Curve on COVID-19", April 15, 2020.
9   Ministry of Health and Welfare (2016), "The 2015 MERS Outbreak in the Republic of Korea: Learning from MERS".
10  The Government of the Republic of Korea, *Tackling COVID-19 Health, Quarantine and Economic Measures: Korean Experience*, March 31st, 2020.
11  "GVPN is a system through which employees can log onto the government ministry's intranet even outside of their office. No matter where or when they work, employees can carry out administrative duties at home or other locations during business trips in Korea or abroad as long as they can use the internet and have access to the government intranet. G-Drive is a cloud storage system tailored to

public officials working for central administrative agencies". <u>The Republic of Korea (2020), "How Korea Responded to a Pandemic Using ICT Flattening the Curve on COVID-19"</u>.

12  *Yeonhap News*, June 14, 2020, www.yna.co.kr/view/AKR20200612042800530, accessed on March 6, 2021.
13  https://eucrim.eu/news/edpb-guidelines-corona-apps/
14  Lee J. C. (2003). Health care reform in South Korea: success or failure? *American Journal of Public Health*, *93*(1), 48–51.

# 6 Boundary Spanning of Learning

This book has examined Korea's response to COVID-19, focusing mainly on the actors, policies, and technologies involved. There is a need to pause to think about what lessons we are going to take with us into the future regarding COVID-19, specifically in terms of management and policies that were used. As COVID-19 caused an immense global impact, there is a need to thoroughly ensure that important factors and lessons do not become overlooked. Over time, people will likely forget about the impacts that COVID-19 had on the social community beyond public health. This distortion of memory will make it impossible to gather lessons learnt about COVID-19 and also the many people who lost their lives by this infectious disease. In order to ensure that important memories and lessons do not fade, we will have to broaden the horizons of what we should learn.

## 6.1 Beyond Public Health Risks

First, we should not limit our lessons related to public health risks. Let's try to find how ChatGPT evaluates the response to COVID-19 using artificial intelligence (AI) when we ask the question: "Evaluate the COVID-19 responses of Korea".

South Korea's response to the COVID-19 pandemic has been widely regarded as a success. The country implemented a **comprehensive testing and contact tracing program**, as well as **widespread use of face masks**, which helped to slow the spread of the virus. South Korea also set up **drive-through testing centers** and **online systems for reporting symptoms and booking tests**, which made it easier for people to get tested. Additionally, the **government's rapid response and transparent communication** helped to keep the public informed and calm. Despite having a population density similar to that of Italy, South Korea has managed to keep its death rate relatively low, with a total death count of less than 600 by 2021.

DOI: 10.4324/9781003125006-6

It can be seen that most of ChatGPT's memories of its response to COVID-19 are about how effectively it controlled COVID-19. It is mainly focused on the government's policies, and there is no evaluation of how civil society has tried to maintain daily life and overcome the pandemic by sympathizing with others in their difficulties. Also, there is no story to be found about how Korean society wisely overcame various shocks affecting education, cultural life, transportation, economy, sports, and politics through a social safety net and mutual consideration beyond the health crisis.

The evaluation of these COVID-19 responses is similar in other countries. The following is ChatGPT's assessment of the US response. Pointing out the problems of the US response, it revealed the lack of preparedness for disasters, the failure to provide PPE, the lack of appropriate guidelines for testing and quarantine, and the problems in the vaccine supply process. Even in the case of the United States, it can be seen that the response efforts of civil society or each system in responding to COVID-19 are not the core evaluation content.

> The United States' response to the COVID-19 pandemic has been widely criticized. The country has experienced one of the highest death tolls in the world, with over 500,000 deaths reported by 2021.
>
> In the early stages of the outbreak, the United States was criticized for **its lack of preparedness and inadequate response**. There were **shortages of personal protective equipment (PPE)** for healthcare workers and testing supplies, as well as **inconsistent guidelines for testing and quarantine**.
>
> The U.S. government has been criticized for its slow response to the pandemic, and for initially downplaying the threat of the virus. The Trump Administration was criticized for not taking the pandemic seriously enough and for **failing to coordinate an effective national response**.
>
> The United States has also struggled with **vaccine distribution**, with many states facing delays and logistical challenges in getting shots to eligible citizens.
>
> Additionally, the United States has experienced a **significant divide in how the pandemic has been handled between states and municipalities**, with some implementing strict measures, while others have been slower to respond, leading to a patchwork of responses and confusion among citizens.
>
> Overall, the United States' response to the COVID-19 pandemic has been widely criticized for its **slow response, lack of preparedness, and inconsistent guidelines**. The country has experienced one of the highest death tolls in the world, and the vaccine distribution has been uneven and chaotic.

As such, efforts to comprehensively understand the acts of various members of society through a whole community approach to responding to COVID-19 are still not common. This is because COVID-19 remains narrowly understood as a public health problem, and the core problem of response is to reduce health risks. Our memories of this will be strengthened over time. In this book, it was emphasized that Korea's response to COVID-19 was the result of joint efforts by various actors. It was recognized from early days that the risk of COVID-19 was beyond health risks and the government knew that this was not a problem that they could solve alone.

So, what else should Korea learn besides the lessons elated to public health? Although not covered in this book, COVID-19 has provided us with countless experiences. Was it a desirable decision to limit educational opportunities to students who had an extremely low fatality rate? How did cultural artists overcome the difficulties caused by the ban on gatherings? How did individuals and communities deal with the psychological shock caused by COVID-19? Would the burden of childrearing be heavier for working women who had to work from home? We will be able to ask a lot of questions and learn new lessons by reliving our experience of responding to COVID-19. We will have to make efforts to learn more lessons by expanding the horizon of COVID-19 memories beyond health risks to various aspects of everyday life that we tend to forget.

## 6.2 The Challenge of Path Dependency

The aftermath of a disaster often leaves a profound and lasting impression on those affected by it, leading to a heightened sense of memory retention. In cases where a disaster has been successfully addressed or significant policy failures have been resolved, such reinforced memory can result in path dependency. Path dependency refers to the notion that the decisions and actions taken in the past can significantly limit the options available in the future. Thus, a country that perceives itself to have successfully overcome COVID-19 based on citizen autonomy is likely to adopt a similar approach in handling future crises. Conversely, a nation that has previously dealt with a crisis through strong government control may swiftly resort to implementing strict social distancing policies in the event of future disasters.

It is imperative to note the distinction between learning from experience and learning from memory, as well as the importance of reflecting on past experiences through thorough analysis. While memory retention may be useful, it does not always provide an accurate representation of past events. On the other hand, reflecting on past experiences through comprehensive analysis can provide valuable insights and lessons that can guide future policies and actions. However, although critical assessment of past experiences and learning is important, there is no guarantee that the learning will be useful for future disaster responses.

Drawing upon the lessons learned from previous experiences is an essential step toward creating effective disaster response strategies. In this regard, the Korean government was able to learn crucial lessons from its response to the MERS outbreak, which played a critical role in shaping the country's approach toward COVID-19. By analyzing the shortcomings of its previous response, the government identified the importance of rapid testing, tracing of close contacts, and isolation and treatment. Moreover, learning should not be limited to individual levels, but should involve many organizations and civil societies that participated in the response process. If learning remains focused on justifying the government's response or assigning blame to specific individuals or organizations, it can lead to flawed learning. In the case of Korea, a higher level of learning was achieved not by relying on government-led efforts, but through a critical retrospective process by medical experts who participated in the MERS response on the ground. The past experience with MERS thus provided a valuable framework for formulating a quick response manual for COVID-19, given the similarities between the two respiratory infectious diseases. It is essential to exercise caution and avoid succumbing to a success trap. While certain measures may have proven effective in response to one particular disaster, it is important to recognize that their efficacy may not be as significant in the face of other types of disasters, such as the collapse of communication networks, food shortages, or environmental crises.

Another potential pitfall of learning from experiences is the risk of confirmation bias, which occurs when we focus only on experiences that confirm our existing beliefs and assumptions, while ignoring or dismissing those that challenge them. This can lead to a distorted and incomplete understanding of the situation at hand and may result in misguided or ineffective responses. In particular, even seemingly similar disasters or crises may have unique contextual factors that require distinct responses. The confirmation bias hinders us from reflecting on the contextual differences across disasters. To guard against overreliance on past experiences, we must strive to strike a balance between learning from previous experiences and remaining flexible, thus allowing us to avoid the potential pitfalls of path dependency.

An example of path dependency observed in the COVID-19 response is the temperature check policy implemented in Korea. While checking fever was thought to help confirm COVID-19 infection, it was later found to be an unreliable method. Nonetheless, public facilities and multiunit facilities continued to install fever check machines and record individual body temperatures, as it was a symbol of the government's quarantine efforts. Even when scientific evidence was presented that fever checks were ineffective and costly, the government did not change its policy of compulsory temperature checks in Korea. On the contrary, the United States quickly lifted up the temperature screen policy based on new evidence. According to the U.S. CDC, more than 766,000 travelers were screened between January 17 and September 13, 2020. Among them, only 1 case per 85,000 travelers screened were identified in the program.[1] Hence, the US CDC stopped recommending the program in September 2020, and some states and private businesses have also stopped using them. Similarly, the European Centre for Disease Prevention and Control (ECDC) has stated that temperature screening is not an effective method of detecting COVID-19, and many European countries, including Germany and France, have discontinued its use as a screening method as well. However, the Korean government did not change the temperature screen policy for travelers even at the end of 2022. It was not because of the lack of scientific information. The Korean government was aware that the airport temperature screen at Jeju airport was not effective, and it had an analysis result that the proportion of asymptomatic patients consistently increased by 30–50%. The ignorance of such information makes the Korean government adhere to ineffective policies. Path dependency of such policy is somewhat related to the belief that the temperature screen was one of the success factors in dealing with SARS and MERS. These experiences remain as memories that influence future choices. Thus, it is necessary to make active learning efforts at both the national and international levels. Learning from the Korean case and other countries can minimize the path dependency of erroneous policies and shared memory for the international society. This highlights the importance of critically analyzing past experiences to create effective disaster response strategies in the future.

The strong memories left by COVID-19 in the international community are negative memories such as border closure, export bans on quarantine foods, and vaccine monopolization by developed countries. Although the scientific evidence that the effect of border closures was weak, based on ethnocentrism, border closures, and export bans on quarantine goods were widely adopted even in democratic countries. As developed countries preoccupied vaccines, the situation in which developing countries had difficulty accessing them continued for some time. Korea also did not adopt a policy such as banning the export or quarantine items at the beginning, but when each country regulated the export of quarantine items and many citizens in Korea requested a ban on exports, they also banned the export of masks. These shared memories run the risk of being transformed into false lessons as the international community responds to new disasters in the future. If we look at ChatGPT again, its answer to the question 'is the border closing an effective tool in COVID-19 response?', the answer is surprisingly effective. "Border closing can be an effective tool in a COVID-19 response, as it can help to slow the spread of the virus by limiting the movement of people between countries. However, the effectiveness of border closing depends on a number of factors, including how it is implemented, the specific characteristics of the outbreak, and the capacity of the country to enforce and monitor the border measures".

The aforementioned response highlights the necessity for evidence supporting the effectiveness of border closures in containing the spread of COVID-19. Notably, countries that implemented such measures widely experienced rapid transmission rates. Consequently, the proposition that effective domestic quarantine policies may be more persuasive in achieving the desired flattening of the curve is worthy of consideration. It is acknowledged that border closures and stringent social lockdowns may reduce the initial rate of transmission. However, their effectiveness hinges on several prerequisites, including the ability to enforce robust border control measures at the early stages of minimal spread. Additionally, the successful implementation of border closures is contingent upon the capacity of the country to sustain the economic impact of such measures for a prolonged duration. Thus, it is imperative to undertake a serious reevaluation of alternative solutions to combat the spread of COVID-19 in societies with interconnected trade, transportation, and communication networks, rather than solely reinforcing the efficacy of border closures in the short term.

The international community's solidarity suffered a blow due to several factors, including the perceived inadequacy of the World Health Organization's (WHO) response to the COVID-19 pandemic. The WHO declared a pandemic on March 11, 2020, following which criticisms surfaced, arguing that the organization did not actively respond while monitoring the initial spread of the virus in China. Moreover, the then president of the United States, Donald Trump, announced the withdrawal of the United States from the WHO in July 2020. It was challenging to accurately determine the risk of COVID-19, as the WHO lacked an organization to conduct scientific research and had to rely on data provided by China in the initial stages. In this context, the United States did not propose any alternative mechanisms to replace the WHO's role in promoting international cooperation. It is noteworthy that the WHO continues to aid developing countries in vaccine distribution and provides guidance on designing response policies to COVID-19. However, the credibility crisis faced by the WHO is likely to endure even after the COVID-19 pandemic has been surmounted. Given that it is arduous to overcome the pandemic with the efforts of specific countries alone, questions have arisen about the WHO's role in tackling COVID-19. Therefore, it is crucial for the international community to learn balanced lessons through an objective assessment of the WHO's performance in the process of responding to the pandemic.

As the COVID-19 pandemic continues to unfold, each actor participating in the response network is developing their own cognitions and lessons learned. These insights have the potential to inform future disaster management policies and institutions. However, it is important to be mindful of the risk of path dependency, whereby past decisions and events limit future options. To overcome this risk, it is necessary to reflect on and analyze the root causes of the success or failure of response policies. By doing so, we can better understand the factors that contribute to path dependency.

Drawing on the Korean experience, we can identify some of the key factors that contribute to successful response policies. These include effective communication and coordination among stakeholders, early and widespread testing, and clear and consistent messaging from government authorities. By analyzing these factors and their contribution to success, we can begin to develop alternative scenarios and explanations that can help us avoid path dependency.

Ultimately, the success of disaster management policies and institutions will depend on our ability to learn from our experiences and adapt to changing circumstances. By reflecting on our successes and failures, analyzing root causes, and seeking out alternative scenarios, we can reduce the risk of path dependency and create more resilient disaster management policies and institutions that can better respond to future crises.

## Note

1 Dollard P, Griffin I, Berro A, et al. *Risk Assessment and Management of COVID-19 Among Travelers Arriving at Designated U.S. Airports*, January 17–September 13, 2020. MMWR Morb Mortal Wkly Rep 2020;69:1681–1685.

# 7  Conclusions

The disaster response process is fraught with paradoxes, as exemplified by the case of Korea's COVID-19 response. It has been widely recognized that overcoming disasters cannot be accomplished solely by the power of specific ministries, organizations, or individuals. Instead, multiple actors must work collaboratively to address the challenges presented by disasters. However, in the process of responding to COVID-19, countries implemented social distancing policies that led to the isolation of individuals within closely connected social networks. While this approach may have reduced the spread of infectious diseases, it also resulted in significant challenges that reduced the resilience required to solve the various problems presented by the pandemic.

Moreover, despite many countries' belief that closing borders and cities was a viable strategy for slowing the spread of the virus, this approach weakened cooperation between countries, making it more challenging to address the various issues collectively. Even more concerning was the growing desire for an authoritarian and hierarchical approach that required overcoming disasters through the leadership of a strong leader. This phenomenon, known as "rally around the flag", may appear natural since overcoming crises often necessitates strong leadership. However, strong leadership is inherently formed and supported through the interaction of multiple actors, and without democratic legitimacy and citizen support, it is unlikely to be effective in overcoming disasters.

It is evident that unexpected disasters cannot be resolved through perfect planning and well-defined command and control relationships. Assuming a perfectly structured hierarchical situation is not a viable approach to address the complexities and uncertainties presented by disasters. Instead, a collaborative and adaptive approach that emphasizes the interaction and cooperation of multiple actors is necessary to build resilience and effectively respond to disasters.

Korea has demonstrated its ability to respond to infectious disease outbreaks through the development of manuals and disaster response governance frameworks, based on the lessons learned from the Middle East Respiratory Syndrome (MERS) outbreak in 2015. Of course, the outbreak of COVID-19 required a significant revision of these frameworks. Notably, Korea recognized

DOI: 10.4324/9781003125006-7

that the state cannot solve all problems alone and actively sought ideas and cooperation from various stakeholders, including private companies, local governments, civil society, and experts. Private small- and medium-sized enterprises (SMEs) developed the diagnostic kit, and private experts developed the mask app, which was utilized for volunteer work. Private financial institutions provided credit and prepaid card networks to deliver disaster subsidies, and logistic companies played a significant role in delivering relief goods. Private hospitals and numerous volunteers contributed to various quarantine activities, such as patient isolation and vaccination.

Korea adopted committee-based decision-making, where opinions were heard from various ministries, experts, business circles, and stakeholders, centered on the Central Defense Response Headquarters, instead of making decisions directly by the president or the prime minister. To implement agility, flexibility, and transparency in disaster response, it is necessary to internalize the flexible policy network structure formed by actors, relations, and interactions into the existing public administration system.

Efficiency in disaster response is not automatically achieved, as multiple actors interact with each other within the policy network. The coordination of their activities is crucial, given the differences in their information level, incentive structure, and resource availability. Laws and rules dictate what each actor should do in a rapidly changing disaster situation. Therefore, securing a communication channel based on information-sharing is essential for self-organized coordination.

In the case of rapidly increasing confirmed cases, strengthening social distancing policies may seem like a natural response for the government, but this may not be the most appropriate action. The rate of increase in critically ill patients may not be fast, and self-isolation can solve the shortage of health care services when many asymptomatic patients are present. Also, if it is possible to supply additional beds and the number of beds is deemed sufficient, a policy to maintain a stable supply of medical services, rather than social distancing, can be adopted. Appropriate information on the patient's condition must be provided to the government and citizens, and external experts help policy networks find alternative solutions.

Transparency in disclosing information by the government has been instrumental in enabling scientists to analyze the information and present countermeasures actively. Open information through Open API can be instantly analyzed through the collaboration of various experts, highlighting the importance of a technical environment that facilitates open information. The role of the state in the policy network should not be overstated or understated. The state possesses unparalleled manpower, financial resources, and information, as well as the legitimate powers conferred by the Constitution and laws. The role of the state in disaster response is crucial, and the Central Disaster and Safety Headquarters was quickly established in the early stage of the COVID-19 outbreak to secure communication governance within the government.

The prime minister took over the responsibility of the Central Disaster and Safety Countermeasure Headquarters, which was initially in charge of the Ministry of Public Administration and Security. The prime minister collected opinions from the heads of various ministries and local governments and decided on important policies related to quarantine. The ability to share and coordinate opinions among various actors is critical, and the Central Disaster and Safety Countermeasure Headquarter provided a space for consultation and cooperation between ministries. The prime minister emphasized communication and cooperation rather than authoritative leadership, as no department had a clear solution, and it was unclear which department would benefit in this situation.

In order to facilitate the collaboration of multiple actors, regulations and administrative procedures made in everyday situations should be reduced so that innovative ideas can be reflected in actual policies. When creating a new medicine, it was impossible to develop a diagnostic kit in three weeks and make a vaccine in less than a year at the moment when numerous regulations that had to be passed to approve it existed as they were. In Korea, telemedicine was in a difficult situation due to the collective resistance of doctors, but these regulations were relaxed because of the urgent circumstance. Even when tracing close contacts, it was possible to quickly block close contacts because the regulations of the Personal Information Protection Act were eased. In addition, the process of permitting COVID testing by institutions other than KCDC if they meet certain standards can be said to be an example of simplifying administrative procedures. Of course, negative issues also arose during this process. Policies that were once widely accepted in the COVID-19 response process, such as the mask-wearing policy, show a reluctance to revise or abolish the existing policy even though the COVID-19 situation has improved. This, like a success trap, results in inefficiencies that arise from sticking to a policy that succeeded in a crisis even in a changed environment. Citizens will pay the cost of institutional rigidity if the policies created at the time of COVID-19 are maintained even after the crisis has been overcome, ignoring the basic rights of citizens caused by privacy infringement and social distancing in the process of responding to COVID-19. The rigidity of the bureaucracy is a risk factor that will continue to be a problem not only in responding to COVID-19, but also in the post-COVID-19 society.

The importance of technological innovation was once again confirmed in the process of responding to COVID-19. Online lectures, remote work, real-time identification and management of COVID outbreaks, provision of disaster subsidies to tens of millions of people at the same time, vaccination, and various emergencies have made it possible to disseminate information because of advances in information communication technologies. Through online commerce, citizens are more likely to procure daily necessities, and the reason why they were able to digest the exponential logistics delivery volume without too much difficulty was because there was an automated logistics classification system and a computer-managed delivery network system. Online lectures were also a simple method of providing recorded lectures in the early days, but based on stable network technology that supports simultaneous access of students and enables mutual discussion, even though the quality of the lectures has begun to improve, even metaverse classrooms have begun to be created. Innovation in medical technology has been proven in the vaccine development process, and the telemedicine system is developing rapidly. In addition, in the development of diagnostic kits, it was possible to shorten the development time very quickly by stimulating various chemical structures using a supercomputer. On the other hand, we also experienced limits of technological innovation. Because the global value chain is so closely linked, problems in procuring small production parts can cause problems throughout the entire production process. A hyper-connected society increases production efficiency and promotes technological innovation, but it can incur huge costs when the network is disconnected. In this respect, it was confirmed that technological innovation not only creates new ways, but also the importance of technological innovations that can increase the stability of existing systems.

Civil society autonomy is the biggest characteristic of the Korean COVID-19 response process. In the process of responding to COVID-19, quite a number of people thought that citizens would not follow important policies such as wearing masks, personal quarantine, self-isolation, and vaccination. In addition, during the spread of Daegu in February 2020, when COVID-19 fears reached their peak, it was thought that there would be great social confusion, such as the spread of hoarding. Surprisingly, however, citizens voluntarily wore masks even before the government's mandatory mask-wearing policy, and the number of self-quarantine violators was less than 1%. Moreover, it showed a surprisingly calm response from the use of a loss income system for personal quarantine to voluntary examinations. Vaccination also showed a vaccination rate of over 90% by the end of 2021 despite side effects. More notably, these actions were preemptive rather than compulsory by the government. For example, citizens already voluntarily reduced their movement quickly before the government announced a policy to restrict the use of multiunit facilities due to the rapid spread of COVID-19. Moreover, even when the government maintained distancing regulations despite the easing of the spread, mobility was restored to normal in a variety of ways.

Not only did citizens move faster than the government policy, but there were very few cases of deviant behavior that threatened the interests of the community for personal gain, as the government feared. Because of the autonomous efforts of civil society, the government was able to avoid resorting to extreme policies such as city blockades.

There were also limits to civil society. In the early days of COVID-19, the existence of xenophobia led to a rapid increase in claims to ban Chinese entry. In addition, when a confirmed case occurred, there were cases where the personal information of the confirmed person was found and disclosed. There have also been situations where even the media has sympathized with social criticism of the confirmed case. Furthermore, in the process of political polarization and confrontation between the ruling party and the opposition party intensifying, civil society also showed a phenomenon in which the viewpoint on quarantine policy changed according to the political orientation. Citizens supporting the conservation opposition party criticized the government's liberal quarantine policy and supported strong social distancing policies. On the other hand, citizens supporting the ruling party supported the government's disaster subsidy support policy or expanded fiscal spending. It is necessary that civil society itself is composed of heterogeneous groups, not a single social organization. It would be inappropriate to claim that the role of civil society should be reduced just because limits exist. This is because the democracy and effectiveness of disaster response can be greatly increased when civil society overcomes its limitations and acquires the capacity to solve problems.

Another thing to note in the process of responding to COVID-19 is cooperation between countries. Just as COVID-19 that occurred in China quickly spread around the world, various COVID-19 mutant viruses that occurred in India, the United Kingdom, and the United States quickly spread to other countries as well. COVID-19 response would have been more difficult if countries did not share information about the mutant virus with each other. In addition, it was easy to formulate a response strategy because information on the fatality rate and severity rate could be obtained while sharing treatment information for confirmed patients in each country. Vaccine development was done quickly with the capital and technology of developed countries, so other countries could also benefit from it. Above all, when China abandoned its Zero-COVID policy and opened its borders in early 2023, the world was concerned that China would re-proliferate the virus around the world. Fortunately, that has not happened, but even if one country is not properly quarantined, the entire interconnected world could be at risk. The importance of quarantine cooperation between developed and developing countries has become more evident in the pandemic situation.

The COVID-19 pandemic has caused immense human suffering, economic hardship, and social distress, the consequences of which will linger long in memory. In order to overcome the crisis, a collective community approach is required, as social distancing measures alone cannot ensure success. Government must therefore work in tandem with the civil society, leveraging social networks to jointly tackle the problems posed by the pandemic. Although Korea has transitioned from a dictatorship to a democratic government three decades ago, there are still many who cling to the notion of a strong, centralized administration. Nonetheless, the response to COVID-19 has revealed the potential for a new disaster response model centered on citizen autonomy. The K-Quarantine model is noteworthy not only for its technical superiority based on 3T (trace–test–treat), but also for its implementation of an autonomous-based disaster response that has not been introduced in Europe or the United States. Moving forward, the post-COVID Korean administration stands to glean valuable insights from the experience of COVID-19, with a greater appreciation for the role of citizen autonomy in disaster response.

# References

Anderson, P. (1999). Perspective: Complexity theory and organization science. *Organization Science, 10*(3), 216–232. https://doi.org/10.1287/orsc.10.3.216

Ansell, C., & Gash, A. (2008). Collaborative governance in theory and practice. *Journal of Public Administration Research and Theory, 18*(4), 543–571. https://doi.org/10.1093/jopart/mum032

Argyris, C. (1991). The use of knowledge as a test for theory: The case of public administration. *Journal of Public Administration Research and Theory, 1*(3), 337–354. https://www.jstor.org/stable/1181917

Argyris, C. (1993). *Knowledge for action: A guide to overcoming barriers to organizational change*. San Francisco, CA: Jossey-Bass Inc.

Argyris, C., & Schön, D. (1978). Organizational learning: A theory of action prospective. Pennsylvania, PA: Addison-Westly.

Avritzer, L., & Rennó, L. (2021). The pandemic and the crisis of democracy in Brazil. *Journal of Politics in Latin America, 13*(3), 442–457. https://doi.org/10.1177/1866802X211022362

Axelrod, R., & Cohen, M. D. (1999). *Harnessing complexity: Organizational implications of a scientific frontier*. New York: The Free Press.

Bajardi, P., Poletto, C., Ramasco, J. J., Tizzoni, M., Colizza, V., & Vespignani, A. (2011). Human mobility networks, travel restrictions, and the global spread of 2009 H1N1 pandemic. *PLOS One, 6*(1), 1–8. https://doi.org/10.1371/journal.pone.0016591

Bardach, E. (1998). *Getting agencies to work together: The practice and theory of managerial craftsmanship*. Washington, DC: Brookings Institution Press.

Barzelay, M. (2001). *The new public management: Improving research and policy dialogue*. Berkeley, CA: University of California Press.

Baumgartner, F. R., & Jones, B. D. (1993). *Agendas and instability in American politics*. Chicago, IL: University of Chicago Press.

BBC News. (2020, February 3). Coronavirus: China accuses US of causing panic and 'spreading fear'. *BBC News*. Retrieved February 24, 2023, from https://www.bbc.co.uk/news/world-asia-china-51353279

Bettis, R. A., & Prahalad, C. K. (1995). The dominant logic: Retrospective and extension. *Strategic Management Journal, 16*(1), 5–14. https://doi.org/10.1002/smj.4250160104

Bevir, M. (2006). The life, death, and resurrection of British governance. *Australian Journal of Public Administration, 1*(65), 59–69. https://escholarship.org/uc/item/0939t2bh

Bevir, M., & Rhodes, R. A. (2007). Decentred theory, change and network governance. In E. Sørensen & J. Torfing (Eds.), *Theories of democratic network governance* (pp. 77–91). Palgrave Macmillan.

Bevir, M. (2008). *Key concepts in governance*. Berkeley, CA: Sage Publications Ltd.

Birkland, T. A. (1997). *After disaster: Agenda setting, public policy, and focusing events*. Washington, DC: Georgetown University Press.

Blau, P. M. (1964). *Exchange and power in social life*. New York: John Wiley and Sons.

Boersma, K., Ferguson, J., Groenewegen, P., & Wolbers, J. (2014, May). Beyond the myth of control: Toward network switching in disaster management. *ISCRAM, 11*, 125–129.

Boin, A. t Hart, P., Sterm, E., & Sundelius, B. (2005). *The politics of crisis management*. New York: Cambridge University Press.

Boin, A., Kuipers, S., & Overdijk, W. (2013). Leadership in times of crisis: A framework for assessment. *International Review of Public Administration, 18*(1), 79–91. https://doi.org/10.1080/12294659.2013.10805241

Brownstein, J. S., Wolfe, C. J., & Mandl, K. D. (2006). Empirical evidence for the effect of airline travel on inter-regional influenza spread in the United States. *PLOS Medicine, 3*(10), 1826–1835. https://doi.org/10.1371/journal.pmed.0030401

Carling, A. H. (1991). *Social division*. London and New York: Verso Books.

Chinazzi, M., Davis, J. T., Ajelli, M., Gioannini, C., Litvinova, M., Merler, S., … Vespignani, A. (2020). The effect of travel restrictions on the spread of the 2019 novel coronavirus (COVID-19) outbreak. *Science, 368*(6489), 395–400. https://doi.org/10.1126/science.aba9757

Chiva-Gómez, R. (2003). The facilitating factors for organizational learning: Bringing ideas from complex adaptive systems. *Knowledge and Process Management, 10*(2), 99–114. https://doi.org/10.1002/kpm.168

Cohn, A. (2005, May 19). FEMA's new challenges. *Washington Times*. Retrieved February 24, 2023, from https://www.washingtontimes.com/news/2005/may/19/20050519-092940-4501r/

Coleman, J. S. (2017). *Mathematics of collective action*. New York: Routledge.

Comfort, L. K. (Ed.). (1988). *Managing disaster: Strategies and policy perspectives*. Durham, NC: Duke University Press.

Comfort, L. K. (2007). Crisis management in hindsight: Cognition, communication, coordination, and control. *Public Administration Review, 67*, 189–197. https://doi.org/10.1111/j.1540-6210.2007.00827.x

Comfort, L. K. (1999). *Shared risk: Complex systems in seismic response, 1999*. Pittsburgh, PA: Pergamon.

Comfort, L. K. (2019). *The dynamics of risk: Changing technologies and collective action in seismic events*. Princeton, NJ: Princeton University Press.

Comfort, L. K., Kapucu, N., Ko, K., Menoni, S., & Siciliano, M. (2020). Crisis decision-making on a global scale: Transition from cognition to collective action under threat of COVID-19. *Public Administration Review, 80*(4), 616–622. https://doi.org/10.1111/puar.13252

Comfort, L. K., Ko, K., & Zagorecki, A. (2004). Coordination in rapidly evolving disaster response systems. *American Behavioral Scientist, 48*(3), 295–311. https://doi.org/10.1177/0002764204268987

Comfort, L. K., Woods, T. R., & Nesbitt, J. E. (1989). *Designing and emergency information system: The Pittsburgh experience*. Berkeley, CA: Institute of Governmental Studies.

Cooper, B. S., Pitman, R. J., Edmunds, W. J., & Gay, N. J. (2006). Delaying the international spread of pandemic influenza. *PLOS Medicine, 3*(6), 0845–0855, e212. https://doi.org/10.1371/journal.pmed.0030212

Corbett, J., Christian Grube, D., Caroline Lovell, H., & James Scott, R. (2020). *Institutional memory as storytelling: How networked government remembers.* Cambridge: Cambridge University Press.

Crosby, B. C., & Bryson, J. M. (2005). A leadership framework for cross-sector collaboration. *Public Management Review, 7*(2), 177–201. https://doi.org/10.1080/14719030500090519

Crossan, M. M., Lane, H. W., White, R. E., & Djurfeldt, L. (1995). Organizational learning: Dimensions for a theory. *International Journal of Organizational Analysis, 3*(4), 337–360. https://doi.org/10.1108/eb028835

Curtis, R. (2008). Katrina and the waves: Bad organization, natural evil or the State. *Culture and Organization, 14*(2), 113–133. https://doi.org/10.1080/14759550802079234

Daft, R. L., & Weick, K. E. (1984). Toward a model of organizations as interpretation systems. *Academy of Management Review, 9*(2), 284–295. https://doi.org/10.5465/amr.1984.4277657

Danescu, E. (2019). *Democracy facing global challenges: V-DEM annual democracy report 2019* University of Gothenburg. Retrieved February 24, 2023, from https://orbilu.uni.lu/bitstream/10993/43444/1/V-Dem_Democracy_Report_2019.pdf

Denhardt, J. V., & Denhardt, R. B. (2015). The new public service revisited. *Public Administration Review, 75*(5), 664–672. https://doi.org/10.1111/puar.12347

El Sawy, O. A., Gomes, G. M., & Gonzalez, M. V. (1986). Preserving institutional memory: The management of history as an organizational resource. *Academy of Management Proceedings, 1*(1), 118–122. https://doi.org/10.5465/ambpp.1986.4980227

Enroth, H. (2011). Policy network theory. In M. Bevir (Ed.), *The SAGE handbook of governance* (pp. 19–35). Berkeley, CA: SAGE Publication.

Feiock, R. C. (2013). The institutional collective action framework. *Policy Studies Journal, 41*(3), 397–425. https://doi.org/10.1111/psj.12023

Ferlie, E., Fitzgerald, L., & Pettigrew, A. (1996). *The new public management in action.* New York: Oxford University Press.

Fong, M. W., Gao, H., Wong, J. Y., Xiao, J., Shiu, E. Y., Ryu, S., & Cowling, B. J. (2020). Nonpharmaceutical measures for pandemic influenza in nonhealthcare settings—Social distancing measures. *Emerging Infectious Diseases, 26*(5), 976–984. https://doi.org/10.3201/eid2605.190995

Fraser, C., Riley, S., Anderson, R. M., & Ferguson, N. M. (2004). Factors that make an infectious disease outbreak controllable. *Proceedings of the National Academy of Sciences, 101*(16), 6146–6151. https://doi.org/10.1073/pnas.0307506101

Freedom House. (2020). *Freedom in the world 2020: A leaderless struggle for democracy.* Freedom House. Retrieved February 24, 2023, from https://freedomhouse.org/report/freedom-world/2020/leaderless-struggle-democracy

Fukumoto, E., & Bozeman, B. (2019). Public values theory: What is missing? *The American Review of Public Administration, 49*(6), 635–648. https://doi.org/10.1177/0275074018814244

Gell-Mann, M. (1994). Complex adaptive systems. In G. Cowan, D. Pines, & D. Meltzer (Eds.), *Complexity: Metaphors, models, and reality* (pp. 17–45). Boston, MA: Addison-Wesley.

Germann, T. C., Kadau, K., Longini Jr., I. M., & Macken, C. A. (2006). Mitigation strategies for pandemic influenza in the United States. *Proceedings of the National Academy of Sciences, 103*(15), 5935–5940. https://doi.org/10.1073/pnas .0601266103

Goldsmith, S., & Eggers, W. (2004). *Government by network: The new public management imperative.* Washington, DC: Brookings Institution Press.

Gostin, L. O., & Lucey, D. (2015). Middle East respiratory syndrome: A global health challenge. *JAMA, 314*(8), 771–772. https://doi.org/10.1001/jama.2015.7646

Ha, K. M. (2016). A lesson learned from the MERS outbreak in South Korea in 2015. *Journal of Hospital Infection, 92*(3), 232–234. https://doi.org/10.1016/j.jhin.2015 .10.004

Heath, A., & Heath, L. E. (1976). *Rational choice and social exchange: A critique of exchange theory.* New York: Cambridge University Press.

Heclo, H. (1978). Issue networks and the executive establishment. In A. King (Ed.), *The new American political system* (pp. 262–287). Washington, DC: American Enterprise Institute.

Hodges, L. R., & Larra, M. D. (2021). Emergency management as a complex adaptive system. *Journal of Business Continuity and Emergency Planning, 14*(4), 354–368. https://EconPapers.repec.org/RePEc:aza:jbcep0:y:2021:v:14:i:4:p:354-368

Hutchins, E. (1995). *Cognition in the wild.* Cambridge, MA: MIT Press.

Ji, Y. (2020). *Public health responses to the COVID-19 outbreak.* Korea: Institute of Public Administration, Graduate School of Public Administration, Seoul National University.

Kahneman, D., Slovic, S. P., Slovic, P., & Tversky, A. (1982). *Judgment under uncertainty: Heuristics and biases.* Cambridge: Cambridge University Press.

Kapucu, N., Arslan, T., & Demiroz, F. (2010). Collaborative emergency management and national emergency management network. *Disaster Prevention and Management: An International Journal, 19*(4), 452–468. https://doi.org/10.1108/09653561011 070376

Kemmelmeier, M., & Jami, W. A. (2021). Mask wearing as cultural behavior: An investigation across 45 US states during the COVID-19 pandemic. *Frontiers in Psychology, 12*, 1–24. https://doi.org/10.3389/fpsyg.2021.648692

KDCA. (2020). Organization. Retrieved April 24, 2023, from https://www.kdca.go.kr/ contents.es?mid=a30107000000

Kim, R., Shin, H., & Kim, P. (2013). Intercrisis learning in disaster response network: Experience of Korea from MERS and COVID-19. *Asian Journal of Political Science*, 1–23. https://doi.org/10.1080/02185377.2022.2157295

Kim, K. H., Tandi, T. E., Choi, J. W., Moon, J. M., & Kim, M. S. (2017). Middle East respiratory syndrome coronavirus (MERS-CoV) outbreak in South Korea, 2015: Epidemiology, characteristics and public health implications. *Journal of Hospital Infection, 95*(2), 207–213. http://doi.org/10.1016/J.JHIN.2016.10.008

Kingdon, J. W. (1984). *Agenda, alternatives and public policies.* New York: Harper Collins.

Klein, G. A. (1993). A recognition-primed decision (RPD) model of rapid decision making. In J. Orasanu, R. Calderwood & C. E. Zsambok (Eds.), *Decision making in action: Models and methods* (pp. 138–147). NJ: Ablex.

Knoke, D., & Kuklinski, J. H. (1982). *Network analysis.* Beverly Hills, CA: SAGE Publishing.

Ko, K. (2007). The review of studies on policy network and the application of social network analysis. *Korean Journal of Public Administration*, *45*(1), 137–164. https://s-space.snu.ac.kr/handle/10371/70390

Ko, K., Chang, S., & Lee, S. (2022). Impact of inter-crisis learning on the risk cognition and the utilization of information technologies in Korea. In L. K. Comfort & M. L. Rhodes (Eds.), *Global risk management the role of collective cognition in response to COVID-19* (pp. 65–83). New York: Routledge.

Ko, K., & Hong, M. (2020). Estimation of impact of comprehensive tests of the COVID-19 in South Korea: Benefit-cost analysis using the extended SEIR model. *Journal of Policy Studies*, *35*(3), 141–168.

Korea Institute of Local Administration. (2020). *Diagnosis and challenges of Local Government's response to infectious disease disasters.*

KOTI. (2020). COVID-19 and its impact on transportation and logistics. Retrieved April 24, 2023, from https://www.koti.re.kr/main/covid19/, accessed on February 23, 2021.

Kraemer, M. U., Yang, C. H., Gutierrez, B., Wu, C. H., Klein, B., Pigott, D. M., … Scarpino, S. V. (2020). The effect of human mobility and control measures on the COVID-19 epidemic in China. *Science*, *368*(6490), 493–497. https://doi.org/10.1126/science.abb4218

La Porte, T. R. (2015). *Organized social complexity: Challenge to politics and policy.* Princeton, NJ: Princeton University Press.

Lagadec, P. (1990). *States of emergency: Technological failures and social destabilization.* London: Butterworth-Heinemann Ltd.

Lee, J. C. (2003). Health care reform in South Korea: Success or failure? *American Journal of Public Health*, *93*(1), 48–51.

Lee, M. H., Park, G., Lee, D., Choi, Y.-I., Oh, Y., & Jang, Y. (2020). *South Korea's responses to COVID-19: Factors behind.* Science and Technology Policy Institute (STEPI).

Lee, J - Y.., Lee, J.-H., & Kim, Y.-H. (2021). A study on the e-governance network in the development process of public mask applications for COVID-19. *Information Policy*, *28*(3), 23–48. https://doi.org/10.22693/NIAIP.2021.28.3.023

Levitt, B., & March, J. G. (1988). Organizational learning. *Annual Review of Sociology*, *14*(1), 319–338. https://doi.org/10.1146/annurev.so.14.080188.001535

Lindblom, C. E. (1959). The science of "muddling through". *Public Administration Review*, *19*(2), 79–88. https://doi.org/10.2307/973677

Lindblom, C. E., & Cohen, D. K. (1979). *Usable knowledge: Social science and social problem solving.* London: Yale University Press.

Linder, S. H., & Peters, B. G. (1990). An institutional approach to the theory of policy-making: The role of guidance mechanisms in policy formulation. *Journal of Theoretical Politics*, *2*(1), 59–83. https://doi.org/10.1177/0951692890002001003

Mackinnon, A. J., & Wearing, A. J. (1980). Complexity and decision making. *Behavioral Science*, *25*(4), 285–296. https://doi.org/10.1002/bs.3830250405

Mandell, M., & Keast, R. L. (2007). Evaluating network arrangements: Toward revised performance measures. *Public Performance and Management Review*, *30*(4), 574–597. https://doi.org/10.2753/PMR1530-9576300406

March, J. S., & Simon, H. A. (1958). *Organizations.* New York: Wiley.

Marsh, D., & Rhodes, R. A. W. (1992). *Policy networks in British government.* Oxford: Clarendon Press.

Marsh, D., & Smith, M. (2000). Understanding policy networks: Towards a dialectical approach. *Political Studies, 48*(1), 4–21. https://doi.org/10.1111/1467-9248.00247

McGuire, M. (2011). Network management. In M. Bevir (Ed.), *The SAGE handbook of governance* (pp. 436–453). Berkeley, CA: SAGE Publication.

Ministry of Health and Welfare. (2016). The 2015 MERS outbreak in the Republic of Korea: Learning from MERS. Korea Institute for Health and Social Affairs. Retrieved February 24, 2023, from https://www.kihasa.re.kr/publish/report/view?type=policy&seq=28860

MOHW. (2020). For entrants to Korea: Instructions for quarantine subjects. Retrived April 24, 2023, from https://overseas.mofa.go.kr/

MOHW. (2020). Korean government's response system. Retrieved April 24, 2023, from https://ncov.kdca.go.kr/en/baroView.do?brdId=11&brdGubun=111&dataGubun=&ncvContSeq=&contSeq=&board_id=

Montpetit, E. (2002). Policy networks, federal arrangements, and the development of environmental regulations: A comparison of the Canadian and American agricultural sectors. *Governance, 15*(1), 1–20. https://doi.org/10.1111/1468-0491.00177

Morris, J. C., Morris, E. D., & Jones, D. M. (2007). Reaching for the philosopher's stone: Contingent coordination and the military's response to Hurricane Katrina. *Public Administration Review, 67*(1), 94–106. https://doi.org/10.1111/j.1540-6210.2007.00818.x

Mousavi, S. (2018). What do heuristics have to do with policymaking? *Journal of Behavioral Economics for Policy, 2*(1), 69–74. https://doi.org/10.2139/ssrn.3164225

Moynihan, D. P. (2005, June 1). *Leveraging collaborative networks in infrequent emergency situations.* IBM Center for the Business of Government. Retrieved February 24, 2023, from https://ssrn.com/abstract=3508158

Moynihan, D. P. (2008). Learning under uncertainty: Networks in crisis management. *Public Administration Review, 68*(2), 350–365. https://doi.org/10.1111/j.1540-6210.2007.00867.x

Moynihan, D. P. (2009). The network governance of crisis response: Case studies of incident command systems. *Journal of Public Administration Research and Theory, 19*(4), 895–915. https://doi.org/10.1093/jopart/mun033

MSIT (Ministry of Science and ICT). (2020). Publicly-distributed face mask information service (March 10). Retrieved March 10, 2020, from http://english.msip.go.kr/english/msipContents/contentsView.do?cateId=tst56&artId=2805542

National Health Insurance Service. Retrived April 24, 2023, from https://www.nhis.or.kr/english/wbheaa02300m01.do

Nisbett, R. E., & Ross, L. (1980). *Human inference: Strategies and shortcomings of social judgment.* Hoboken, NJ: Prentice-Hall.

OECD/KDI. (2018). *Understanding the drivers of trust in government institutions in Korea.* Paris: OECD Publishing. https://doi.org/10.1787/9789264308992-en

OECD. (2020). *OECD reviews of public health: Korea.* Paris: OECD Publishing. https://doi.org/10.1787/b5788ba4-en

Olson, M. (1965). *The logic of collective action.* Cambridge, MA: Harvard University Press.

Ostrom, E. (1998). A behavioral approach to the rational choice theory of collective action: Presidential address, American Political Science Association, 1997. *American Political Science Review, 92*(1), 1–22. https://doi.org/10.2307/2585925

Pappas, P. G., Kauffman, C. A., Andes, D., Benjamin Jr. , D. K., Calandra, T. F., Edwards Jr. , J. E., ... Infectious Diseases Society of America. (2009). Clinical practice guidelines for the management of candidiasis: 2009 update by the infectious diseases society of America. *Clinical Infectious Diseases: An Official Publication of the Infectious Diseases Society of America, 48*(5), 503–535. https://doi.org/10.1086/596757

Park, S., Choi, G. J., & Ko, H. (2020). Information technology–based tracing strategy in response to COVID-19 in South Korea—Privacy controversies. *JAMA, 323*(21), 2129–2130. https://doi.org/10.1001/jama.2020.6602

Perrow, C. (1984). *Normal accidents: Living with high-risk technologies.* Princeton, NJ: Princeton University Press.

Pierre, J. (2000). *Debating governance: Authority, steering, and democracy.* Oxford: Oxford University Press.

Pressman, J. L., & Wildavsky, A. (1984). *Implementation: How great expectations in Washington are dashed in Oakland; or, why it's amazing that federal programs work at all, this being a saga of the economic development administration as told by two sympathetic observers who seek to build morals on a foundation.* Berkeley, CA: University of California Press.

Quarantelli, E. L., & Dynes, R. R. (1977). Response to social crisis and disaster. *Annual Review of Sociology, 3*(1), 23–49. https://doi.org/10.1146/annurev.so.03.080177.000323

Quarantelli, E. L., Lagadec, P., & Boin, A. (2007). A heuristic approach to future disasters and crises: New, old, and in-between types. In W. A. Andersson, P. A. Kennedy, & E. Ressler (Eds.), *Handbook of disaster research* (pp. 16–41). New York: Springer.

Rinaldi, S. M., Peerenboom, J. P., & Kelly, T. K. (2001). Identifying, understanding, and analyzing critical infrastructure interdependencies. *IEEE Control Systems Magazine, 21*(6), 11–25. https://doi.org/10.1109/37.969131

Ryu, S., Hwang, Y., Yoon, H., & Chun, B. (2022). Self-quarantine noncompliance during the COVID-19 pandemic in South Korea. *Disaster Medicine and Public Health Preparedness, 16*(2), 464–467. https://doi.org/10.1017/dmp.2020.374

Sabatier, P. A. (1988). An advocacy coalition framework of policy change and the role of policy-oriented learning therein. *Policy Sciences, 21*(2–3), 129–168. https://doi.org/10.1007/BF00136406

Sabatier, P. A. (1999). *Theories of the policy process.* Boulder, CO: Westview Press.

Schulz, M. (2017). Organizational learning. In J. A. Baum (Ed.), *The Blackwell companion to organizations* (pp. 415–441). Oxford: Blackwell Business.

Scott, J. (2000). Rational choice theory. In J. Scott, J. Browning, A. Halcli, & F. Webster (Eds.), *Understanding contemporary society: Theories of the present* (pp. 126–138). London: Sage Publications.

Shaw, R. B., & Perkins, D. (1992). *Organizational architecture.* San Francisco, CA: Jossey.

Sherman, H. J., & Schultz, R. (1999). *Open boundaries: Creating business innovation through complexity.* New York: Basic Books.

Simon, H. (1982). *The sciences of the artificial.* Cambridge, MA: The MIT Press.

Simon, H. A. (1990). Bounded rationality. In J. Eatwell, M. Milgate, & P. Newman (Eds.), *The new Palgrave: Utility and probability* (pp. 15–18). London: WW Norton & Company.

Stacey, R. D. (1996). *Complexity and creativity in organizations.* San Francisco, CA: Berrett-Koehler Publishers.

The Government of the Republic of Korea. (2020, April 15). *Flattening the curve on COVID-19: How Korea responded to a pandemic using ICT.* The Government of the Republic of Korea. Retrieved February 24, 2023, from https://overseas.mofa.go .kr/gr-en/brd/m_6940/view.do?seq=761548 p.8

Tian, H., Liu, Y., Li, Y., Wu, C. H., Chen, B., Kraemer, M. U., ... Dye, C. (2020). An investigation of transmission control measures during the first 50 days of the COVID-19 epidemic in China. *Science, 368*(6491), 638–642. https://doi.org/10 .1126/science.abb6105

Tierney, K., Bevc, C., & Kuligowski, E. (2006). Metaphors matter: Disaster myths, media frames, and their consequences in Hurricane Katrina. *Annals of the American Academy of Political and Social Science, 604*(1), 57–81. https://doi.org/10.1177 /0002716205285589

Waugh, W. L. (2003). Terrorism, homeland security and the national emergency management network. *Public Organization Review, 3*(4), 373–385. https://doi.org /10.1023/B:PORJ.0000004815.29497.e5

Wegner, D. M. (1995). A computer network model of human transactive memory. *Social Cognition, 13*(3), 319–339. https://doi.org/10.1521/soco.1995.13.3.319

Weick, K. E. (1988). Enacted sensemaking in crisis situations. *Journal of Management Studies, 25*(4), 305–317. https://doi.org/10.1111/j.1467-6486.1988.tb00039.x

Weick, K. E. (1995). *Sensemaking in organizations.* Thousand Oaks, CA: SAGE Publications.

Weick, K. E., Sutcliffe, K. M., & Obstfeld, D. (2005). Organizing and the process of sensemaking. *Organization Science, 16*(4), 409–421. https://doi.org/10.1287/orsc .1050.0133

WHO. (2020). Infection prevention and control for the safe management of a dead body in the context of COVID-19. *Interim Guidance.* Retrieved from https://apps.who. int/iris/bitstream/handle/10665/331538/WHO-COVID-19-IPC_DBMgmt-2020.1- eng.pdf

Wildavsky, A. B. (1979). *Speaking truth to power: The art and craft of policy analysis.* Boston, MA: Little, Brown & Company.

Worldometer. (2020, April 18). DR Congo: Coronavirus cases. *Worldometer.* Retrieved February 24, 2023, from https://www.worldometers.info/coronavirus/country/ democratic-republic-of-the-congo/

Yeonhap News. (2020, June 12). 자가격리 무단이탈자 총 531명...안심밴드 착용자 누적 116명. *Yeonhap News.* Retrived April 24, 2023, from https://www.yna.co.kr/ view/AKR20200612042800530

# Index